THE
CONTROL
FREAK
REVOLUTION

Make Your Most Maddening Behaviors
Work for Your Company and to Your
Advantage

By Cheryl Cran

CAREER
PRESS

Franklin Lakes, NJ

Copyright © 2008 by Cheryl Cran

THE CONTROL FREAK REVOLUTION
EDITED BY JODI BRANDON
TYPESET BY EILEEN DOW MUNSON
Cover design by Design Works Group
Illustrations on pages 32, 50, 67, 85, 116, 146, 150, 195, and 208
courtesy of Mike Baldwin
Mike Baldwin © 2007
Distributed by Universal Press Syndicate
Printed in the U.S.A. by Book-mart Press

To order this title, please call toll-free 1-800-CAREER-1 (NJ and Canada: 201-848-0310) to order using VISA or MasterCard, or for further information on books from Career Press.

The Career Press, Inc., 3 Tice Road, PO Box 687,
Franklin Lakes, NJ 07417
www.careerpress.com

Library of Congress Cataloging-in-Publication Data

Cran, Cheryl, 1963-
    The Control freak revolution : make your most maddening behaviors work for your company and to your advantage / by Cheryl Cran.
        p. cm.
    Includes index.
    ISBN-13: 978-1-56414-984-8
    ISBN-10: 1-56414-984-6
        1. Leadership. 2. Personnel management. 3. Control (Psychology) 4. Interpersonal relations. I. Title.
HD57.7.C696 2008
650.1—dc22

                                                                    2007031665

*I would like to dedicate this book
to two men
who have been the most impactful in my life:
my dad
and
my wonderful husband,
Reg.*

Acknowledgments

There are many people involved in the production of one book. I would like to acknowledge first my husband, Reg, who is my rock, my biggest fan, and my best friend. My daughter, Courtney, for her enthusiastic belief in all I do, and my two stepsons, Tyler and Jordan, for their love and encouragement.

A special mention to my agent, Arnold, my editor, Jodi Brandon, and the team at Career Press. I also want to acknowledge Karen Harris and her team at CMI Speaker Management.

Thank goodness for my friends. They have helped to keep me light, have fun, and enjoy the process. Here's to Sue, Sharlae, Jay, Colleen, and all of my colleagues who are writers and speakers.

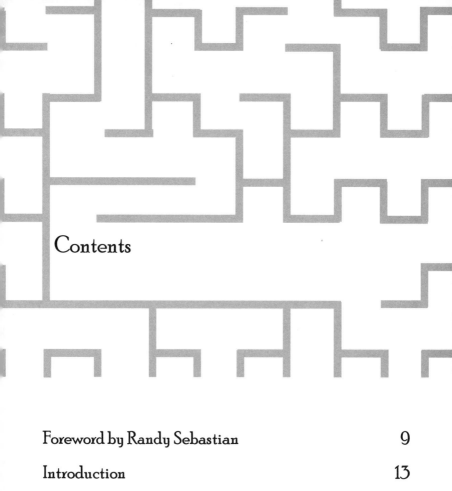

Contents

Foreword by Randy Sebastian   9

Introduction   13

Chapter One: 15
    Own Your Inner Control Freak

Chapter Two: 35
    Shift or Get Off the Pot

Chapter Three: 55
    Funky Control Freak or Freaky Control Freak?

Chapter Four: 73
    Set Up Your Control Panel

Chapter Five: 91
    Personalities, Cultures, and Generations—
    Oh My! Conflict and the Control Freak

Chapter Six: 111
    Myths and Maddening Behaviors

Chapter Seven: 131
    7 Steps to Be a Successful "Control Freak" Leader

Chapter Eight: 149
    Control Freaks: Let Others Evaluate You

Chapter Nine: 179
    Make Your Most Maddening Behaviors Work
    for You

Chapter Ten: 199
    Leadership With Positive Control of Self and
    Others

Bibliography   213

Index   215

About the Author   223

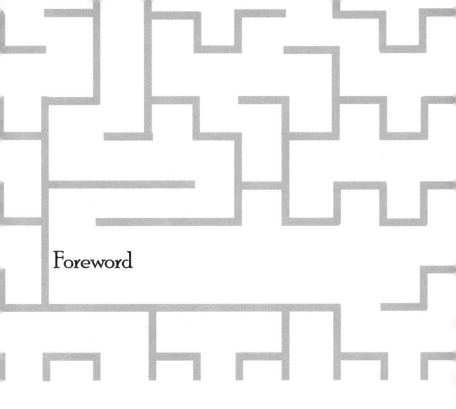

Foreword

Control Freak Builds 100-Million-Dollar Business!

It was more than 20 years ago when I founded Renaissance Homes and began my new construction business building custom, luxury homes. Renaissance Homes' early market niche proved to be a fortuitous choice, as it created a company culture of pride in everything we do: unique locations, innovative plans, quality materials, and uncompromising craftsmanship. It's a culture that naturally flows to our clients, so they can feel pride of ownership every day they live in their Renaissance home. Today Renaissance Homes has grown to be one of the Portland area's larger and most respected builders.

Award-Winning Homes

Renaissance Homes has won the prestigious "Best of Show" award at Portland's annual Street of Dreams four times—more times than any other builder. Here's why these awards are so important to new home buyers: Awards are the collective opinions of experts and prospective buyers confirming that what we have designed and built is as functional as it is beautiful.

It means we try harder and are more successful at creating homes that are more desirable and more fun to be in, which is why we look at every new home plan and ask, "How does this home *live?*"

Renaissance Earth Advantage

We're always looking for better ways to build homes. Joining the Earth Advantage Green program is an ideal example. Today, Renaissance Homes is the largest local builder building 100 percent green. In fact, we've even exceeded the green building specifications.

Our success as a company is directly related to the leadership culture we have established. We encourage our leaders to be "funky control freaks." In my opinion, my business has grown in proportion to the talented control freaks we have within the organization.

When I started my business I wanted to build unique and top-notch homes that would attract buyers who appreciate quality and attention to detail. My personal area of control freak was around quality, process, and customer satisfaction.

In my opinion our customers love the fact that I and my entire team are all control freaks when it comes to quality, process, and service. Want to get something done? Give it to a control freak who has learned how to do something really well and then has learned how to attract the right people who have the same level of control freakiness.

I have worked with Cheryl for two years now, and her keynotes, training programs, and consulting processes for improved leadership have helped us to double our earnings.

In addition she has helped us to keep our best people and develop our leaders to own their inner control freak in a positive way that has impacted our business exponentially.

Am I a proud control freak? You bet. Who do I hang with? Other highly productive, strongly opinionated, and very successful control freaks.

I strongly urge you to read this book to learn more about how to be a highly effective funky control freak. Whether you are someone who resists control or someone who tends to over control this book will help you to differentiate between good and not so good control freakiness.

From one proud control freak to another. All the best.

Randy Sebastian

CEO, Renaissance Development

Portland, Oregon

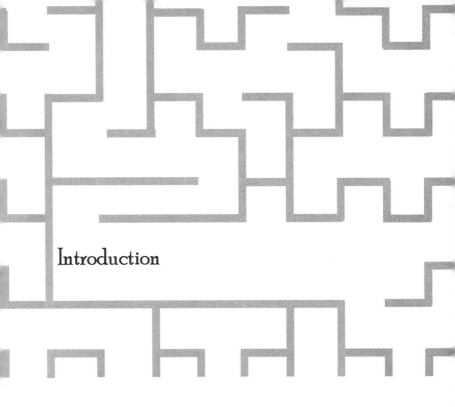

Introduction

Of course you don't need this book—but you or someone you know does!

If you think about it, everyone wants control. We want control of our lives, our future, and our happiness. In fact psychologists state that happiness is directly related to the amount of perceived control one has over their life.

For some reason the term *control freak* has become more and more common. We hear it when Penelope Cruz decides she wants to reshoot a scent in her movie. We hear it when Donald Trump says he won't do another season of *The Apprentice* without more control. But are these so-called "control freaks" really doing anything wrong?

It seems to me that there are the types of control freaks that we admire and aspire to be like. The type of control that is inspiring is control over self, discipline, and focus- and action-oriented behavior toward success.

The "control freak" who is not appreciated is the overbearing, arrogant, and condescending person who has the need to over control and over manage due to his/her own insecurity.

I felt it was important in this book to distinguish between the negative control freak and the positive control freak.

We are in a control freak revolution as a society. People want to control their lives with technology and work-life balance, and to be happy. Leaders need to be what I call "funky control freaks" in order to be respected and to produce the results that their company needs.

This book tackles the behaviors of a control freak, emphasizes the behaviors that we want to develop, and points out the behaviors that are not appreciated by others and will cause them to label us a "control freak" with the negative edge.

Learn to own your inner control freak, to make the shifts you need to change your behaviors, and how to be freaky (not good) or funky (great!). You will find questionnaires, your very own control panel, how to influence others through heightened awareness of cultures, personalities, and generational differences. Discover the myths and maddening behaviors that can limit your success. Finally, through letting others evaluate you and how to make your maddening behaviors work, you will discover the seven steps to being a successful control freak leader who has positive control over self and others.

Enjoy!

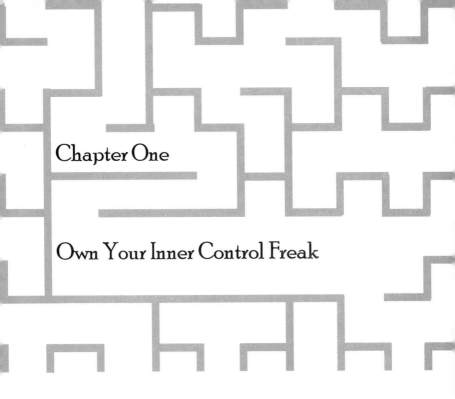

Chapter One

Own Your Inner Control Freak

Control your destiny or somebody else will.

—Jack Welch

Have you ever had a gun held to your head?

Imagine that one day you are minding your own business working in banking customer care, and all of a sudden two guys with masks and sawed-off shotguns come bursting through the side door. They order everyone to the floor, and you stand there in complete shock. One of the gunmen comes up to you, puts his gun to your head, and says, "I said get to the floor!" You, being somewhat sarcastic under pressure, say, "Why didn't you say so in the first place?" and you get to the floor. While you are on the floor you have two thoughts: *Man, am I stupid* and *We really need to clean these carpets.*

When the robbery is over you get up without thinking, and you look over and see your boss cowering in the corner, people crying, and mass bedlam. You quickly take control; you dial 911 and check on the tellers to make sure they are okay. When the police arrive you provide descriptions and explain the entire robbery. In a situation of sheer terror you took complete control.

If you were in a life-or-death situation would you want to be with someone who took control?

In an Australian survey dated May 2, 2006, 385 employees from around the world responded to a survey titled "Is You're Boss a Control Freak?" Sixty-eight percent had a male boss; 32 percent had a female boss. Interestingly, 68 percent of employees with a female boss considered her to be a control freak, whereas 57 percent of employees with a male boss considered him to be a control freak.

Control freaks have been given a bad rap. When we hear the term *control freak* we often picture someone who is up-tight, rigid, and overly controlling. Control freaks come in many forms, and many behaviors fall within the control freak definition. For example, being a passive communicator can be controlling, withholding information from employees is controlling, and refusing to take time off is highly controlling. The time is now to clarify the positive aspects of being in control and to weed out the negative components.

We are in what I call a **Control Freak Revolution**.

Now more than ever we need to have leaders who are willing to take positive control, to have high levels of self-control, to set up systems that positively control project completion, and to focus on what they CAN control rather than waste energy on what they cannot control.

Think of famous leaders such as Rudy Giuliani, Donald Trump, Martha Stewart, Oprah Winfrey, and Barbara Walters to name a few. What do they all have in common? They are all control freaks at some level. This has served them very well and made them very successful, and a lot of their success can be attributed to being somewhat of a control freak. None of them waited for someone to take control for them, and not one of them blamed their setbacks on others or on circumstances beyond their control—instead they all quite clearly took control by the horns and rode the bull all the way to their current levels of success.

Oprah's story is classic. She had a childhood of victimization and, rather than be tormented or immobilized by the events of her life, she took control of her thought, control of her choices, and control of her behaviors to get her to where she is today.

> *We are each responsible for our own life—no other person is or even can be.*

> —Oprah Winfrey

Society is actually encouraging us to take control. Think about it: We are all trapped by time constraints, and many of us want to take control of situations in order to speed things up; for example, Home Depot recently installed self-serve check-out kiosks for those who do not want to wait in line for a cashier to process their transaction. Target, Wal-Mart, and other retail outlets have implemented the same system because they have recognized that a large demographic of the public wants to "control" the speed and payment of their transactions.

We are given more control when we go to Starbucks and order our black tea latte, no classic syrup, one pump sugar-free vanilla soy latte. We are being encouraged by our environment to take more control.

Have you noticed that when other people do not respond to our needs with speed, attention, or care we tend to lose control?

I am on a mission to set the record straight about the negative connotations of being a control freak. The Control Freak Revolution is about to begin—a revolution to clarify when being a control freak is a good thing. A revolution to have us all recognize the negative control freak attributes and to build on our control freak strengths for even greater success, results, and, yes, control over our lives.

A great pleasure in life is doing what people say you cannot do.

—Walter Bagehot

Own your inner control freak.

The first step in owning your inner control freak is to recognize what we actually have control over and what we do not. Here's a snapshot:

What We Control	What We Cannot Control
Our thoughts.	Other people's thoughts.
Our choices.	Other people's choices.
Our actions.	Other people's actions.
	Everything else!

Now some of you reading this might be thinking, *Yes, we can control other's thoughts, choices, and actions. Just look at the media.* That's exactly the point: Media can influence our thoughts, and you can influence other people's thoughts, choices, and actions, but we certainly cannot control them. We do want to positively influence others so that there is a greater chance of them following us, believing us, and taking action to support our requests.

We are all control freaks on some level. Come on—admit it.

If you are still in denial about this, answer the following questions with a yes or no answer.

Control Freak Questionnaire

Yes	No	
☐	☐	I am highly effective at what I do.
☐	☐	No one else can do what I do.
☐	☐	If I don't do it, it won't get done.
☐	☐	I just keep my mouth shut and let others do the talking.
☐	☐	I go along with what they say and do my own thing.
☐	☐	I worry that I can't do all the work I have.
☐	☐	When others let me down I get angry.
☐	☐	I do not like to delegate.
☐	☐	It's faster to do it myself.
☐	☐	Everything has to be perfect.
☐	☐	I worry that it won't get done right.
☐	☐	I will agree to do another project even though I am swamped.
☐	☐	I do not ask for help when I am swamped.
☐	☐	When my boss asks how I am doing I always say great.
☐	☐	When my boss asks how I am doing I always say busy.
☐	☐	I expect others to understand me.
☐	☐	I feel like a glorified babysitter.
☐	☐	I take pride in never taking a vacation.
___	___	Totals

If you answered yes to three or less, you are a mild control freak. Keep reading and pass this book along to someone else when you are done.

If you answered yes to six or more, you are a moderate control freak. Keep reading and focus on your positive control freak tendencies.

If you answered yes to nine or more, you are a strong control freak. Keep reading very, very carefully.

Positive control freaks are "funky"; negative control freaks are just plain "freaky."

The Monday Morning Test

Which of these Monday morning scenarios describes you the best?

Scenario #1

You come in to work on a Monday morning. You head straight for your office ducking your head and hoping that no one will stop to chat with you. You have no time. You have things to do, people to talk to, and people to meet.

Scenario #2

You go in to work on a Monday morning. You ask everyone how their weekend was, and you do the office stroll to get caught up on everyone's life. It takes you a while to buckle down and get started on the week's work.

Scenario #3

You arrive at work quietly and head to the lunchroom to put away your lunch. You look through the newspaper for a few minutes, you read the bulletin board to see if there is any company news, and then you head straight to your computer with your head down and open your e-mail to see what's up for the day.

Do you think any of these scenarios could be perceived by others as controlling?

The first scenario could be viewed as controlling, as our sole focus is to ignore our team and get straight to work. We may not be consciously ignoring our team, but that is how it could be perceived. If we have evolved into an alert and aware control freak we will have recognized the potential negative perception by others, joked about our Monday morning behavior to everyone in a self-aware way to normalize it, and then adapted ourselves to take the time to say good morning, socialize a little bit, and then get to work.

What we may perceive as efficiency others may perceive as controlling or anti-social; everyone's perception is their reality. We want to shape positive perceptions to create greater success and results.

When I was in my first leadership position in my early 20s I was the type of person described in Scenario #1. Why? Because it was my innate nature to always be in a rush, always have important things to do, and always have no time for chit-chat because what I was working on was so important. I was not a bad person; I was a highly effective person who got lots of work done, got superb results, and didn't have many friends at work. My behavior was perceived as controlling to others because I was not taking the time to connect with my coworkers, which gave them a negative perception. On the other hand, in my mind I was taking control of my environment so that I could focus on output. Whose perception was right?

The answer is both. I had to learn to take a few minutes on a Monday morning to say good morning to my coworkers, chat a little bit about the weekend, and then say, "Well, it was great to catch up. I have so much to get started on, I'll touch base with you later."

Some of you may be reading this and thinking that we can't control others' perceptions of us; that would be an erroneous thought. We can influence others' thoughts about us, and we want to behave in ways that provide positive perceptions—not negative perceptions—without changing the core of who we are. Thus lays the trick in becoming a positive control freak.

We want to focus on control behaviors that are perceived as positive while maintaining integrity with who we are.

Scenario #2 could be perceived as controlling as well. You are controlling when you will actually get to work. It could be perceived that you are preventing others from getting to their work and that you are displaying a lack of control and discipline. Now think about this from a team perspective. Do we want to be perceived negatively? I don't think that is anyone's goal, but our unconscious behaviors can contribute to others having a negative perception of us. You could still be who you are, but also be alert and aware as a control freak as to how your behavior could be perceived. You could then adjust it so that it is working for you and not against you. So in this scenario you could do your quick visits, state that you have lots to get started on, and say you will catch up with him/her throughout the day.

Scenario #3 could also be perceived as controlling. You are quietly entering the workplace, and with your internal behavior it could be viewed as you withdrawing or not wanting to engage. The difference between Scenario #1 and Scenario #3 is that you are not even wanting to look at anyone, let alone interact with them, until you have had at least one cup of coffee and some alone time. There is nothing wrong with each of our own rituals, BUT we need to be open with others about our behavior so that they can accept it rather than make their own negative assumptions about it.

In all three scenarios having an awareness of our Monday morning behaviors frees us up to be self-effacing and to poke fun at ourselves while setting expectations with our coworkers that we are not purposely trying to be controlling. Rather, we are simply easing in to the workweek our own way. The next step of course is communicating our quirks and tendencies openly, honestly, and with humor to those we work with so that we create an environment of trust, safety, and freedom for everyone to be who they truly are.

3 Types of Control

There are three different types of control freakiness that contribute to the possibility of negative perceptions and being labeled a control freak with a negative connotation: overt control freak, covert control freak, and alert and funky control freak.

The goal is to "out" the overt and covert behaviors, and focus on being an alert and aware control freak.

When we use the overt control freak and covert control freak behaviors, they create negative freaky perceptions, which can be perceived as controlling. The goal is to become alert and aware as a control freak or a funky control freak so that we can maintain high levels of positive control while creating positive perceptions and behaviors from those around us.

Let's look at the overt control freak beliefs and behaviors and how they can contribute to negative perceptions by others.

The Overt Control Freak (Perceived as a Freaky Control Freak)

People who are overt in their control freakiness have the beliefs shown in the chart on page 24, which results in behaviors based on the accompanying beliefs.

You can see from the list of beliefs and behaviors that these behaviors are not pleasant to receive. Also, if we are truthful and we use overt control freak behaviors, you can see that the thoughts behind the behaviors are often subconscious, and we may not even be aware that those thoughts are the driving forces behind the resultant behaviors.

Belief	Behavior
I am better than you.	Highly controlling.
You are less than me.	Condescending.
You move too slow for me.	Overbearing.
You aren't listening to me.	Loud voice/sometimes yelling.
You can't do it as well as I can.	Takes away the project.
Why am I the only one who gets it?	Superiority.

The reason an overt control freak is controlling is because he/she has a conscious or unconscious desire to prove to the world that he/she is indeed valuable. When someone behaves this way it is difficult for others to form a connection or to feel respect.

You will notice that people around you are afraid of you, will not feel safe to discuss their jobs with you, and will leave you out of team activities because they feel intimidated by you and ultimately do not like you.

Do not underestimate the likeability factor when it comes to success in the workplace. Although we are not in a popularity contest it is important to note that leaders and workers who are liked typically get greater recognition and opportunities.

I know because I stand before you as a recovering overt control freak!

I believed early on in my leadership career that the only way to get ahead was to be aggressive, which overt control freak behavior is. I thought I was being assertive because I was action-oriented and wasn't afraid to speak my mind. It wasn't until I had a brave boss who had the courage to give me tough feedback that I recognized that my behavior was going to cut my career aspirations short. My boss at the time, Ron, called me in to his office for our quarterly coaching meetings. (This was back in the 1980s when having a boss do quarterly coaching was fairly innovative.) Ron started out asking me some questions about how I thought I was doing in my role as leader at the bank. He asked me what I thought my coworkers thought of me and I answered, "I think they think I am hardworking and that I get good results." Ron's response floored me. He said, "Cheryl, you are hardworking, and you do get great client results. However, you are like a bull in a china shop, and your coworkers do not like you." Now, you have to know that this was not easy to hear, and I wouldn't have been able to hear it if Ron hadn't been the kind of boss who I respected greatly. It was Ron who told me when he hired me that his goal was to have me one day surpass him in my career. Because he had such high regard for me I could hear his difficult feedback. I sat there and said to myself, "I am not going to cry. I am not going to cry." And when I left his office I went to the ladies room and I cried. I was angry; I went home to my husband of more than 20 years and said, "Can you believe the audacity of Ron to tell me I am like a bull in a china shop?" My husband, Reg, just raised his eyebrows and began to whistle. Yikes! Twice in one day I was given feedback that no overt control freak ever wants to hear— I wasn't as good as I thought I was in my self-inflated sense of self. What a great lesson, though, in curtailing negative control freak behavior that could have shortened my successful career. I went back to Ron the next day and told him that I didn't like the feedback, but because I respected him I could hear it and wanted his advice on what to do about it. Ron suggested a course on communication and leadership and, when I went to that course I recognized I was not only aggressive, but I was off the charts!

I acquired tools to work on being alert and aware, and from that turning point in my career at the age of 24 I poured my heart and soul into how to be the best communicator and leader I could be. It is interesting that my perceived weakness at the time turned out to be a great strength; my consultant career has been based on helping others to be stronger leaders and communicators.

How to Deal With an Overt Control Freak

When on the receiving end of overt control freak behavior there are two ways of handling it. The first is to stand up to him/her and the second is to appeal to the ego. Neither of these responses is easy to implement and requires tremendous courage and assertive ability.

Stand up to overt controlling behavior.

Overt control freaks roll right over people. Often they do not even recognize the destructiveness of their behavior until someone has the courage to point it out to them.

Shortly after I was sent to that communication and leadership course I mentioned, I came back and had a meeting with my team. I said to my team, "I guess I haven't been that easy to work for, huh?" Everyone looked at me and nodded their heads. Lela, my assistant at the time, had the courage to stand up to me and said, "You know, Cheryl, we know you are busy and don't like interruptions, but if you could just let us have a chance when we approach you, not interrupt us, and let us finish, then I know it would be easier for me." Wow. That must have taken a lot of courage for Lela to say, and again the others just sat there and nodded their heads.

Suddenly I had newfound respect for Lela, and I said, "Lela, I am willing to do that, and can I ask you and the rest of the team to do me a favor?" Lela said, "Sure. What is it?" The whole team leaned forward to hear what I was going to ask and I said, "The next time any of you want to ask me something could you please think of what you are going to say in three sentences or less?" Everyone laughed, it eased the tension, and I had now brought out into the open my awareness of my negative behavior, and a willingness to change and grow. Lela had a sense of humor, and in the next hour she came into my office and said, "Cheryl, customer, lobby." Three words! Hallelujah—that was music to my ears. Because of her willingness to speak the truth and stand up to my behavior, I was willing to admit, change, and then have a sense of humor as we all moved forward.

Once you stand up to an overt control freak he/she sees you as someone who has conviction and his/her respect goes up. He/she then sees you as being on par with him/her and in turn will behave less aggressively. How do you stand up to him/her? Use this three-step process:

1. Assert your position.
2. Reaffirm his/her position.
3. State the action moving forward.

Lela used that process to confront me successfully. Here is another example of using that three-step process:

→ı Jane, I am going to have to disagree with you on how this project is to be managed. With my strength in long-term planning I believe we need to relook at our time lines and outcomes.

→ı I know you have tremendous skill in projects of this nature and have managed them for some time. I respect that, and I would like equal respect in my opinion of how to have us manage this project successfully for both of us.

→ı I have prepared a sample project management time line of my own to demonstrate the alternatives in moving forward with this. Let's discuss.

Using the three-step process example, what we are doing is asserting our own strength and position while also respecting Jane's strengths and position. The outcome is that we now move forward to discuss how to revamp the project time line so that we are both happy with it.

Appeal to the ego.

The second way of handling highly overt control freaks is to appeal to the ego, which many of us just don't want to do. The important thing to note, though, is that it works. When appealing to the ego, ensure that you are centered and sincere, or else it will come across as patronizing, and that will send the aggressive person into a rage. An example of appealing to the ego is another client I worked with recently on an 18-month consulting project in developing systems around leadership management, human resources, and performance review implementation. The CFO of this $100 million construction company is one of the most intelligent people I have encountered. Tim has vast experience from years of being in a large corporate environment and is largely responsible for the growth of the company he now heads up as CFO. Tim does not suffer fools lightly and has no time for people who have not done their homework.

When I was hired as a consultant I was hired by the CEO, Randy. Randy was sold on my abilities because he had seen me present at a conference in San Francisco on leadership and employee satisfaction. In the first meeting where I was to meet Tim he walked in, quite blustery, in the middle of the executive briefing I was conducting. Randy had already given me the lowdown on Tim and his modus operandi. When Tim walked in I simply continued the briefing. I looked up to acknowledge him, but then continued. After we went around the boardroom table our last person was Tim.

His behavior was very controlled and controlling, and he began to go on about what the company needed, what it didn't have, and why focusing on leadership was premature. I simply picked up my pen and took copious notes in my notebook. I let him talk for about 20 minutes nonstop, nodded my head, and kept writing notes. When he was finished talking I said, "Well, it's obvious why this company has done so well in the last six years that you have been here. It's because you have the brilliant ability to see what needs to be done, who needs to do it, and how it needs to be done for optimal results." He sat back and looked at me without speaking, and I went on, "It seems to me that of the seven items you listed as imperative to moving forward, four are already being handled and the three outstanding are directly linked to what I bring to the table." At that point Tim's entire demeanor changed and he leaned forward and said to me, "I like you." That's it. I was hired. He and I have gone toe to toe more than once, and it has been wonderful.

The two ways of handling overt control freak behavior—stand up to him/her and appeal to his/her ego—both work exceedingly well. Give them a go.

Covert Control Freaks (Perceived as Freaky Control Freaks)

People who display covert control freak behaviors have the beliefs shown in the chart on page 30, which results in behaviors based on the accompanying beliefs.

These behaviors are controlling and can be the most difficult to deal with.

Many of us don't even know that we are using covert behaviors until it is pointed out to us. For example, for the ladies reading this right now: If you are ever asked by your family what you would like for your birthday and you respond with, "Oh, nothing. Your love is all I need," that would be covert.

Belief	Behavior
What if I get found out?	Secretive.
I can do it alone.	Manipulative.
I want the recognition for me.	Controlling.
I can't trust anyone.	Says one thing to your face and another behind your back.
I can't say what I really want.	Makes you feel guilty.
It's not my fault.	Someone else is to blame, or silence.

Why? Because it is a lie. Secretly we are disappointed when on our birthday we either get what we asked for, which is nothing, or we get a lame gift.

My husband, Reg, just had a birthday, and he is difficult to buy for because he is particular about what he wants. This makes it a challenge to buy gifts for him. I bought him two shirts in a brand he likes, and two pairs of pants in a brand that fits him well and that he likes. The day of his birthday I waited while he unwrapped his presents to see, first, if he would like them and, second, if they would fit. It turns out that three of the items did not fit. Luckily that day we were heading to the same shopping center where I had purchased the items, so we could go and exchange them.

However, after he unwrapped his gifts I said, "It is so frustrating to try and buy something for you because inevitably we have to do an exchange." He said, "Oh, honey, it's the thought that counts." Now, my husband is a very smart man.

He has a degree in conflict and mediation and our house can often appear as if we are all in a dysfunctional *Frasier* episode. As soon as he said that I laughed and said, "Liar! We both know that you wanted those items to fit you." He laughed, too, and admitted the truth. Covert behavior is nontruthful, and therefore it is controlling in a negative way.

It is important to recognize that we can all be covert at some point, and it is equally important to recognize that it never works, as it is manipulative and nonrespectful. There are two ways to best deal with someone who is covert. The first is to call him/her out and speak the truth. The second is to strongly confront him/her and give him/her choice.

Call him/her out and speak to the truth.

Many of us will fall back to covert control freak behaviors when we do not want to face the truth or we are afraid of how we will be viewed. A good example is children who learned to blame their brother or sister for something rather than own up to something they did themselves. I have a daughter who is 19 and two stepsons who are 27 and 25. Kids can be good at this behavior unless it is pointed out that it is unacceptable behavior that abdicates responsibility. Courtney, my daughter, now knows that she cannot blame other people or circumstances for something she simply did or didn't do. When she was growing up we would point out her role in the situation and help her to see that blaming others is a victim approach and never works in the long run.

It is also far easier to talk the truth, tell the truth, and deal with the truth then it is to continually support a lie. Supporting a lie takes massive amounts of energy and eventually will get found out. For example, let's say you have someone at work who seems to be different or not behaving as his/her normal self. You ask him how he's doing today, and he responds with "fine." This is a lie; we want to call out the truth because if there is something wrong we can deal with it and prevent a larger problem later on. When we call out the truth we want to do it in a way that is supportive and caring, so our response to the employee's "fine" answer could be, "You know, John, you just don't seem your normal self today. Let's take a few moments and talk about what's going on." Usually the person with the covert control freak behavior will respond positively to our concern because he/she can sense that we are coming from a caring place. If he refuses to sit down and tell the truth, simply respond with, "Okay, John. I won't press it. If you need to talk later, just let me know. I am going to check in with you, okay?"

Cornered   by Mike Baldwin

5-2   © 2007 Mike Baldwin / Dist. by Universal Press Syndicate www.cornered.com
cornered@comic.com

"Since the operation, the slightest thing sets him off."

Confront and give him/her choice.

The second effective way of dealing with covert control freak behavior is to confront them and give them choice. This is difficult for those who dislike confronting, and yet highly effective at putting a stop to continual covert tendencies. Typically people who are covert are also highly defensive. They are insecure and so, when placed in a situation where they may have to truthfully look at themselves, they will push back. I worked with a coaching client a short while ago who hired me to coach her so that she could be more effective as a leader. Sophie had been given feedback from her boss that she was isolated from her team and not connected. He recommended she get some coaching centered around communication and team interaction. Sophie was again highly effective at what she did, got great results, and yet was not perceived positively by her team. She was perceived as a snob, a non-team-player, and someone who was superior to her coworkers.

This upset Sophie greatly, as she did not see herself that way at all. She saw herself as reliable, efficient, and results-oriented. One of the first processes in working with coaching clients is a self-assessment, and Sophie resisted doing that first assignment from the beginning of our working together. I interview everyone I coach prior to taking them on, and I had clearly stated to her that all assignments had to be tackled with truth and commitment—and she had agreed. Yet here we were at the very first assignment and she was pushing back. Often passive aggressive people will simply not do what they are asked to do, which is a form of manipulation. So the method I had to use with Sophie was to confront and offer choice. I gently confronted her by saying, "Sophie, you have a desire to become a better leader, to be more connected to your team, and to take a look at limiting behaviors that may be holding you back right?"

Sophie agreed, and then I said, "Sophie, because you made a commitment to both yourself and to me, I am not willing to let you dishonor that commitment so I am going to give you two choices. First, you can admit you are afraid to complete the self-assessment because you may not look as accomplished as you would like, and then take action and complete the self-assessment so that we can meet your goals of the coaching. Second, you can quit the coaching process, and go back to your former behaviors and the results those behaviors got you. It's your choice." When put this way, Sophie made the choice that was more difficult, but she knew the full accountability of the situation was squarely on her shoulders.

When dealing with a covert control freak or a freaky control freak it can literally feel as though we have a gun to our head. In the bank robbery story at the beginning of this chapter I got promoted for using control in a positive way. I got promoted to the branch with the second-highest robbery rate in the city! Be careful what you are good at.

In Chapter Two we will explore the funky control freak who is alert and aware—the kind we all strive to be.

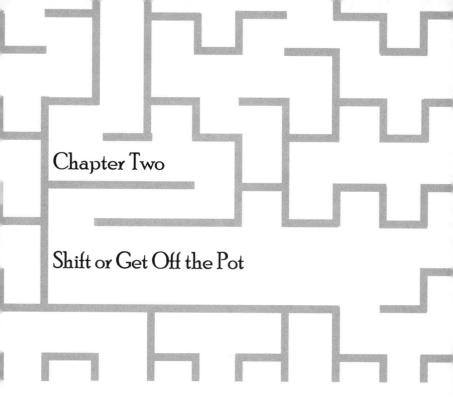

Chapter Two

Shift or Get Off the Pot

It is time for us all to stand and cheer for the doer, the achiever—the one who recognizes the challenge and does something about it.

—Vincent Lombardi

Leaders need new thinking to help them shift into evolved leaders. Leadership by control alone no longer works. In the 1950s the work environment required controlling leaders who could dictate what needed to be done and punish when things were not done correctly. This dictatorial style of leadership worked in a post-war work environment where manual labor was the main form of work. In today's environment we need leaders who are willing to take control in a new and different way.

According to Wikipedia the definition of control freak is:

A control freak is a derogatory term.

In psychology-related slang, control is the attempt to impose excessive predictability and direction on others or on events, often associated with insecurity or a lack of trust. Frequently, a person labeled "a control freak" has a position of authority or superiority in a relationship; however, the person's obsessiveness extends beyond the acceptable range of control. The term is used for extreme cases.

The term *control freak* is often overused and not used properly when we are actually making choices that are in control of our life or in control of guiding a desired outcome. No wonder the control freak is viewed so negatively.

In Chapter One I talked about the overt and the covert control freak (a.k.a. freaky control freak). In this chapter I want to cover the positive attributes of the funky control freak who is alert and aware of his/her thoughts, choices, and behaviors. A *funky control freak* definition on Wikipedia might be:

A funky control freak is a complimentary term.

Funky means good, hip, and fun. Control freak, when used with funky, means someone who is labeled as having complete control over his/her thoughts, actions, and behaviors. He/she does not blame others, he/she takes full responsibility for his/her life, and he/she leads others to take responsibility for their lives. In the workplace the funky control freak is someone with vision, clear goals, open communication, and strong drive to create great results. Typically those who work for and with a funky control freak enjoy his/her candor, self-effacing humor, and ability to take decisive action.

Leadership isn't for wimps, especially in today's relentless business environment. For leaders it is time to shift or become disposable. Although most of North America is currently in an employee's market, where employees are in demand and there is a continuing shortage of workers, companies cannot afford to keep those who cannot lead and execute at high levels.

Harvard Business School professor Teresa Amabile and her team discovered three leader behaviors that do not bring out the best in people:

- → Under- or over-specifying assignments: Either giving too much or too little guidance.
- → Monitoring in a negative form—that is, checking on assigned work too often or not enough, going into too much detail, and giving unconstructive feedback.
- → Avoiding solving problems that crop up in the team or the project and creating problems.

Conversely, the top behaviors that positively support people are:

- → Supporting people emotionally.
- → Monitoring people's work in a particularly positive way. Giving them positive feedback on their work or giving them information that they need in order to do their work better.
- → Recognizing people for good performance, particularly in public settings.
- → Consulting with people on the team by asking for their views, respecting their opinions, and acting on their needs and their wishes.
- → Spending time collaborating with members of the team.

The skills required today include being emotionally resilient, visionary, strategic, empathetic, intuitive, collaborative, and able to exert appropriate control to guide projects and plans to successful completion.

Marcus Buckingham, the author of *Now Discover Your Strengths,* points out that we need to focus on what our strengths are rather than our weaknesses. Someone who is alert and positively controlling has many strengths. Let's take a look at the strengths of a control freak and discover how focusing on the strengths of being a control freak can work for us in surprisingly effective ways:

→ Knows how to get recognition.

→ Is a fast decision-maker.

→ Doesn't wait to take action.

→ Is a risk-taker.

→ Takes responsibility for decisions.

→ Is clear on what he/she wants.

→ Convinces others to go along with ideas.

→ Focus on the strengths.

Knows How to Get Recognition

The strength of a funky control freak is that he/she typically knows how to get recognition for his/her efforts. This is a great skill that gains his/her exposure for his/her contributions, ideas, and efforts. The downside is that others around the control freak who does this are usually holding themselves back from gagging. The control freak may be lacking in the ability to give credit where it is due to teammates, peers, or other contributors.

This reminds me of Donald Trump, the master of getting attention for his endeavors. Recently, when Donald Trump was interviewed about his latest *Apprentice* series, he boldly stated that his show would crush other programming in that same time slot. It struck me that he had an opportunity to talk about how the show would be more successful this time around because of the quality of the contestants or due to the addition of his son and daughter to the show. Instead he stayed focused on himself and his success. If he focused on his strength to gain recognition, but used more creativity and inclusion, it would be easier for others to take and present a more positive and cohesive image to the viewers.

Is a Fast Decision-Maker

When we look at the strengths of a control freak we can see that they are very positive traits. A leader who is a fast decision-maker is a huge asset in today's environment, where offices have the need for speed. If speed alone was all that was needed, then control freaks would be in high demand. An aware and alert control freak needs to learn the art of gathering input quickly, assimilating the information quickly, and then making a decision. The inclusion of others into the decision-making process allows the collaborative process to flourish and provides the funky control freak leader with a positive impact on both the results through the fast decision-making and building a team that respects and values the leader because of their willingness to include others.

A client of mine who is a funky control freak has a habit of making very fast decisions, often without consulting anyone else. He is the CEO so one could argue that this is his right, but I have pointed out to him a few times that, in the wake of his fast decisions without consultation, usually damage control follows from everyone else. Recently the CEO made the decision to hire someone for a department within the company and simply parachuted that person into the department. The aftereffects were felt by all of those within the department, but also by human resources.

The CEO recognized that, had he taken a few moments to float his plan by the other stakeholders, he may have prevented employee backlash, which came in the form of sick leave, bad feelings, and having to adapt without preparation to his decision. The strength of him making this decision is that there was a need for a position to tackle a large segment of that department, and so ultimately it was a great decision for the company. However, the people that it affected had to recover and figure out how to move forward with this new component to their department.

Doesn't Wait to Take Action

Action! A funky control freak is action-oriented. If we go back to the premise that we need to have more control in our lives and we need to be accountable, then we can easily see that being action-oriented is a positive strength of a funky control freak. When we take action and withhold information from others before taking the action, we are in effect operating as a one-woman or one-man show. The response from those around us is to throw up their hands in desperation and futility because they are thinking, *What's the use? He/she is just going to go do it anyway.* There are times when action without consultation is appropriate, but then we need to ensure that we communicate the action and inform those that will be affected by the decision. The times when action without consultation are appropriate may be when there is no one else around to make the call or take the action, and when not taking action could result in a do-or-die scenario for the company. However, freaky control freaks can manipulate this by continually stating that no one was around when a decision was needed, and so this becomes a purely controlling mechanism that is self-serving rather than something that is done for the benefit of the company.

You may or may not be a *Grey's Anatomy* fan. In a recent episode Dr. McDreamy (Patrick Dempsey), a neurosurgeon, was performing a surgery at which a high-level cardiologist was present. Dr. McDreamy made a decision to do an emergency heart massage during the brain surgery. The high-level cardiologist praised him for the quick thinking, but his heart surgeon colleague who was next door was peeved that he had not been called in, as it was his specialty. Control freak? Well, one could argue that he saved the woman's life, and so it was justifiable—or we could argue that he could have called in the heart surgeon and still saved her life, which would have been better for the hospital overall. The point is, action is good, but are we thinking of the bigger picture when we take the fast action?

> *I don't waste time worrying about something I can't control.*

> —Dakota Fanning

Is a Risk-Taker

Alert and aware control freaks are indeed talented at the ability to take risks that others may not have even the slightest amount of courage to initiate. Most of us admire those who can seemingly take risks without fear of loss or repercussion. A great risk-taker is Donald Trump. "Always look out for yourself," says Trump. Never one to back down from a challenge, Trump has made a career out of risk-taking and being ruthless when it came to his business. Trump realized early on that he would only reach the heights of success of which he dreamed if he was willing to tackle whatever or whoever stood in his way. He took no prisoners when it came time to make a deal and did whatever it took to get the job done. When Trump was first getting his feet wet in the Manhattan real estate market in the 1970s, he immediately took a liking to the property at 56th Street and Fifth Avenue, and began designing plans for its renewal. The 11-story building was owned by Genesco, which had also bought out the adjacent Tiffany store. Trump knew that, especially in light of the depression that the market was facing at the time, it was going to be a difficult task to acquire this property.

Repeatedly told that his grandiose plans were unrealistic, Trump refused to give up. "I was relentless, even in the face of total lack of encouragement, because much more often than you'd think, sheer persistence is the difference between success and failure," said Trump. His persistence paid off, and his property would soon be home to the now-famous Trump Tower, a 58-story building, which, with its elaborate décor and indoor waterfall, has become a New York City landmark.

Trump understood that, in order to be successful, he had to ignore his critics and remain headstrong. Unwilling to ever back down, Trump advises, "When somebody challenges you, fight back. Be brutal. Be tough. Just go get them." He attacks all his deals with similar ferocity, refusing to take *no* for an answer.

"My style of deal-making is quite simple and straightforward," says Trump. "I aim very high, and then I just keep pushing and pushing and pushing to get what I'm after. Sometimes I settle for less than I sought, but in most cases I still end up with what I want."

The strength in being a risk-taker is the ability to focus, take control of the situation, and hold steady all the way to the end. Donald Trump admits that he has alienated others along the way and that this is a consequence of his need to dig in and win. He doesn't seem too concerned with this, as he feels that the right people on his team will support his risk ventures.

An alert control freak recognizes that there is great strength in his/her ability to take risks, and he/she also needs to acknowledge that others can be frightened or unsure of taking the same risks without support, guidance, or training.

Takes Responsibility for Decisions

An additional strength of an alert and funky control freak is his/her innate ability to take responsibility for his/her actions. This is a huge strength, as you will not find a funky control freak who will blame others unless he/she indeed did not take personal responsibility for a job or duty. A funky control freak views responsibility as a given. In other words, he/she believes that if he/she can own up to a mistake then he/she expects that others will do the same.

Where a control freak can get freaky with this one is in lack of communication. Due to his/her own ability to take responsibility, he/she can assume (and you and I know what happens when we assume) that everyone is on the same page. The skill that needs to be developed here is mastery in communication. As leaders, we need to ensure that all of our "givens" or expectations are completely communicated at all times. Many control freak leaders can undermine their leadership by simply not communicating to their teams what it is they expect, need, or want. This leaves teams guessing at what the boss might want, and this typically results in letting the control freak leader down, which then results in further negative control freak behaviors.

The funky and alert control freak is fully aware that he/she has a fine-tuned antennae for risk, control, and personal responsibility, and that these three skills are not necessarily in the forefront of awareness for others. Therefore the funky control freak leader needs to consistently communicate his/her behavioral expectations from himself/herself as well as from others. Reward and recognition need to be given when others respond with taking full responsibility, so that others can see that this type of behavior is rewarded and encouraged. This one definitely falls under the "lead by example" rule. An example of this is Martha Stewart and her hands-on style, which clearly shows her willingness to demonstrate what she wants and her expectations of others.

Once a team has been assembled, Stewart maintains a hands-on approach, going to photo shoots, going on sales calls, and going out into the field in order to ensure she is personally involved in the development of her staff and her business. "I view these as important opportunities to share my thought process and to help good employees become great," she says. Stewart also maintains weekly discussion forums with her staff in order to evaluate the business culture and critique each other's work. Though many in her own company have criticized this management style, Stewart feels that it is necessary to change and grow as a company. Otherwise, "when you are through changing, you're through," she warns.

As an entrepreneur, Stewart advises that you need to be willing to adapt to the times. "What worked well last month may suddenly not be working at all," she says. People change, companies change, and it is only the successful manager that is able to reconcile the two. Stewart goes on to say, "I'm a maniacal perfectionist. And if I weren't, I wouldn't have this company.

"I have sometimes, probably, forgotten—and I know I have—to pat the back of someone or said 'thank you' enough times or maybe even once sometimes. I wish I were perfect. I wish I were just the nicest, nicest, nicest person on Earth. But I am a businessperson.... If I were a man no one would ever say that I was arrogant."

The key is that Martha Stewart is completely aware of her style, personality, and modes of operation, and one could argue that she is indeed a funky control freak.

Is Clear on What He/She Wants

A strength that is both rare and admirable is in someone who knows exactly what one wants. Funky control freaks have tremendous amounts of focus. They single-mindedly focus on a goal or an achievement, and with discipline and skill they work toward attaining what they see and what they want. Steve Jobs of Apple is an excellent example of someone who has had vision and clarity about what he wanted for the future.

In 1996, Apple bought neXT for $402 million, bringing Jobs back to the company he founded. In 1997 he became Apple's interim CEO after the directors lost confidence in and ousted then-CEO Gil Amelio in a boardroom coup. In March 1998, in order to concentrate Apple's efforts on returning to profitability, Jobs immediately terminated a number of projects, such as Newton, Cyberdog, and OpenDoc. In the coming months, many employees developed a fear of encountering Jobs while riding in the elevator, afraid that they might not have a job when the doors opened. The reality was that Jobs's summary executions were rare, but a handful of victims was enough to terrorize a whole company. This practice became known as "getting Steved."

We could view Jobs's terminations of projects and people as something a negative control freak would do, or we could view him as someone who was very clear on what he saw, what he wanted, and therefore what he didn't want. I personally believe that it took tremendous courage to pass up other projects and people in order to remain focused on the very vision of what it is he wanted. Of course the people affected by Steve Jobs's decisions would not look favorably upon his choices, but they would also have to admit that the focus and clarity with which Jobs worked has definitely contributed to the success of Apple today. As a leader who is clear on what he/she wants, he/she also does not have fear of dealing with difficult people or situations in order to create a positive outcome. A leader who did not have a healthy grasp on control would not be willing to tackle poor performance or nowhere projects, or be willing to change things in order to create the success that they can so clearly see in his/her mind's eye.

*The universe constantly reminds you that
you're not in control. You're not in charge of
the whole world.*

—Reese Witherspoon

Convinces Others to Go Along With Ideas

A formidable strength of an alert and funky control freak
is his/her ability to convince others to go along with him/her. A
freaky control freak would use manipulation, fear tactics, and
bullying. A funky control freak has learned how to communicate in a way that identifies the needs of others as well as his/
her own needs. Masterful communication requires a win-win
mentality. Funky control freaks acknowledge that, although the
goal is win-win, they need to be okay with being uncomfortable
rather than comfortable when dealing with others. In his book
Reinventing Yourself, Steve Chandler talks about this in a segment titled "Dying Inside Your Comfort Zone":

> The comfort zone is a place to rest, not to live.
> Doug Grant fell from a scaffold on which he
> was working and wound up in the hospital tem-
> porarily paralyzed from the waist down. After
> being in the hospital for a few days he began to
> receive visits from nurses and counselors who
> were trying to help him deal with his situation.
> Doug was getting more and more upset because
> they kept asking him to deal with being para-
> lyzed. That was the last thing he wanted. He
> knew he needed to focus completely on what
> he did want which was to walk again. He had
> to convince the nurses and doctors that he was
> going to walk again and the next person who
> told him to 'deal' with his paralysis would have
> to deal with their own. The point is Doug had

to first convince himself of what he wanted and once he was very clear he knew his next job was to convince those around him so that they would support what he did want. He did walk again and went on to win a gold medal in a weightlifting championship. The gifts of a funky control freak are many if we choose to see them as strengths. In this story Doug took complete control of his mind, his words, and his expectations of others' thoughts and support around him. This is a great example of a funky fully responsible control freak.

Is Stuck in Old-Style Freaky Control Freak Behaviors

The risk of staying in old-style freaky control freak behaviors is that we could conceivably lose our jobs or the promotion we have been hoping for. The strengths of a funky control freak are great when they are met with full awareness and the ability to harness those strengths.

A former client was the CFO of an international company in the technology sector. This company was based in the United States with subsidiaries in other countries. Cindy was highly effective at execution, but alienated others in the company through her leadership style. Her style was autocratic, efficient, and results-oriented. However, she came across as an uncompromising bully. The result of Cindy's style of leading was that her employees were afraid to stand up to her and therefore did not perform to their highest abilities. The CEO and I coached Cindy on balancing her style with a more personal touch and empathy. The shift she needed to make was to balance her leadership style for greater effectiveness. The first step was for Cindy to acknowledge the strengths she brought to the company in her role as CFO. It was evident that her strengths were in the areas of vision, strategy, and getting things done quickly. She was what I would call a classic Driver personality (which I talk about in my first book, *Say What You Mean—Mean What You Say*). The motto of a Driver is "do it and do it now," and the mannerisms are typically gruff, focused on end results but not too overly concerned with other people and their feelings. As a female CFO she argued that if she were a man, she would be highly respected for her direct style. I worked with Cindy to have her realize that the very skills that she considered strengths were preventing her from accessing other skills that would help her get better results from her team. I worked with this organization to facilitate 360-degree performance evaluations where the leaders are evaluated by their peers and their employees via anonymous surveys conducted via the Internet. Once the feedback is compiled I sit down and deliver the results with each leader and manager, and then use the results as the basis for ongoing leadership coaching for development.

When we sat down to deliver Cindy's results it was evident that her team rated her highly in the same areas that she rated herself highly. However in the areas of communication, empathy, and inspiring leadership she fell below the mid-range. This was difficult feedback for her to receive, as Cindy had placed all of her value on her strengths and really didn't see the need to develop these other areas. A freaky control freak doesn't see the need to take anyone else's opinion into account. In his/her mind, if his/her boss is happy, then that is all that matters. This is old-style control freak mindset.

In this chapter we used examples from Donald Trump, Martha Stewart, and Steve Jobs, and their ability to focus on the strengths of a funky control freak. I would bet money, though, that each of them has learned to take feedback, grow, and apply it in order to get to where they are now. All three of them have had difficult and trying times as a result of using funky control freak methods, and all three have come back fresh, new, and somewhat softened in a sense.

In the end Cindy rose to the challenge and saw the connection between her need to be controlling, nontrusting, and overbearing to her team's performance. I was pleased that, when I had finished working with this group, Cindy had shifted her strengths to include adapting to each individual on her team, communicating information that the entire team needed to succeed, and delegating more frequently in order to show trust in her team. Cindy had shifted into evolved thinking and an alert and aware funky control freak.

Have you ever found that what you most need to learn finds you? A number of years ago I had a situation that caused me to realize that I had very little control over external situations but that I had a whole lot of control over my internal thoughts, actions, and behaviors. In fact the following story made it into Richard D. Carlson's *Don't Sweat Stories*. Here's the story, in my own words:

In my career as a speaker, I have traveled to many different places and have been privileged to meet many people. A lot of the events and conferences I have spoken for consist of hardworking folks who have been asked by their companies to meet in order to hear a speaker or to take a training course.

I am familiar with the challenges my audience members have, such as lots of work to do back at the office, I am accustomed to the travel, and I am accustomed to having the majority of my presentations go smoothly. Once in a while a group has its unique challenges.

I was scheduled to speak in Akiachuk, Alaska, to a group of Alaskan villagers on the topic of communication and customer service. Akiachuk, Alaska, is difficult to travel to, and is a very remote part of Alaska. To get there, I flew from Vancouver to Seattle, Seattle to Anchorage, and Anchorage to Bethel. The plan was to stay at a bed-and-breakfast in Bethel and then fly by Cessna to Akiachuk the following morning to do the seminar. It sounded a little different than what I normally would do, which is stay in a hotel and make my way to the client meeting the next morning.

When I arrived in Bethel, the owner of the company was there to meet me and informed me that there was a change in plans. And let me tell you: It was a BIG change in plans.

"Welcome to the Remote Control Freak Recovery Program."

I would be now taking a boat up the Alaskan river, spending the night in Akiachuk, and then flying back by Cessna to Bethel after the seminar. Now, when I say boat, I don't mean a large cruise ship. This was a 6-foot aluminum boat with an outboard motor. It took us two hours of crossing open water to get to the village. I huddled deep inside my warm coat the whole time and prayed that we didn't capsize, as I would have definitely sunk to the bottom with my luggage.

At last we found the village, but I realized I didn't know where I would be staying. No regular bed-and-breakfasts in this town. The CEO who hired me said I would be staying at his place.

Okay. First I have to take a boat to get to the village, and now I have to stay with a complete stranger. This was NOT what I had signed up for. I called my husband (yes, they had TV and phones, but no plumbing), and I told him that I was safe and sound. I told him that I would call him later to let him know I when I was on my way home. I couldn't give him an address other than the village of Akiachuk.

The CEO asked me what I wanted for dinner, and I said I typically eat vegetables and fish. He grinned and said, "Great. We'll catch our dinner later." He handed me gum boots, a fishing rod, and a cap with netting attached.

As I mentioned, the house had no plumbing. As tactfully as possible, he tried to explain the "honeypot" in my room. For those of you who don't have older relatives telling you stories of life before toilets, let's just say it was a chamber pot. This business trip was not turning out quite as I'd expected, and I had a lot to say to the meeting planner who set this one up for me.

I kept mentally reminding myself to stay calm and to focus on the positive. We went fishing for our dinner, and were covered in black flies and mosquitoes. Thank God for the cap with the netting. I didn't catch any fish, and by this time it was 10:00 at night on an August evening. It only gets dark in Alaska in the summertime for about an hour. On our way back to the village, my host ran out of gas. Once that was fixed, we stopped at a fish camp so that I could see what one looked like. When we returned to the boat, it was full of water. By now it was almost midnight. We bailed the water out of the boat before heading back to the village.

We finally had dinner at around midnight. I went to sleep, barricaded my door, slept with my clothes on, got up the next morning, and couldn't shower. No plumbing, remember? I fixed myself the best I could by using hairspray on my bangs (now they stood out like a shelf) and went to do the seminar.

My presentation did not get off to a great start. From the looks on the faces of the folks sitting before me, I could tell I was bombing—big time. During a break, the CEO came to me and asked me to set up a role-playing exercise, thinking that it might help the mood. I wasn't sure it would, but I did it anyway. All hell broke loose in the room, as long-suppressed emotions and issues between coworkers came to the surface. It was a total disaster turned over, with everyone yelling at each other.

At that point I took a deep breath and realized I had to do something different. I decided to try a new approach. I asked everyone to form a circle with their chairs. I used a pool cue as a talking stick, and we threw the workbooks away. For the next two hours we focused on making sure each person was heard. The challenges and emotions that had caused major conflicts were brought to the surface, and solutions were discussed.

After that dreadful start, the seminar did turn out to be a success after all, and I flew as planned by Cessna back to Bethel. My flight home was the following morning. Shortly after take-off, there was an announcement that we would be turning and making an emergency landing back in Bethel because of a fire in the cockpit. Once we were back in the Bethel airport, I walked back in to the small terminal and I broke down in tears.

A sympathetic woman came up to me, put her arm around me, and listened patiently as I poured it all out. It turned out she was an Episcopalian minister.

I finished sobbing out my tale and looked up at her, expecting to see a look of sympathy. Instead, she was smiling and shaking her head. "What a wonderful experience you had! You had to take a small boat to Akiachuk! WHAT an adventure! Yes, you had to use a honeypot. Yes, you had to fish for your dinner, but he cooked it! Yes, you ran out of gas and got stuck on the riverbank, but you got to see an Alaskan fish camp! Yes, your plane had to turn around and you won't be home today, your birthday, but you are alive! Yes, the group did not follow the regular rules of conduct, but you followed your intuition, you honored them, and you were successful! What a blessing you have received."

I listened in disbelief. Could she be right? Was I blessed, and had I been lucky every step of the way—lucky enough to have experienced new and varied things? This event proved to me I could not control many things, but I could control my attitude and how I looked at the things that had happened. It turned out to be a huge learning experience, and let's just say I don't need to fish for my dinner again!

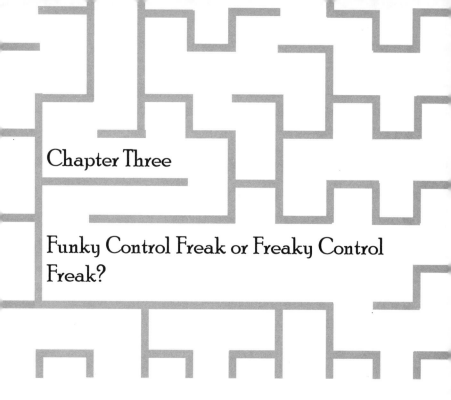

Chapter Three

Funky Control Freak or Freaky Control Freak?

None are so old as those who have outlived enthusiasm.

—Henry David Thoreau

There is nothing better than when clients refer you to one of their top clients because they believe in your services. I always ask my clients for referrals—as a control freak this helps me control whether I stay in business or not. A short time ago a corporate CEO who is one of my customers referred me to one of his top suppliers. Of course my client who referred me to his contact is a high-level control freak, so I thought it likely that the supplier would be a high-level control freak as well.

Here's what I have found: Control freaks usually like to hang out together.

I asked my client to introduce me to his supplier in a joint meeting, but the timing didn't work for my client, so he asked to contact the supplier directly while I was in town. My client, true to his word, had already advised his supplier I would be calling.

As soon as I called the referral lead—let's call him Bob—I could tell I was dealing with an extremely high-level, no-BS control freak. He talked fast, he was abrupt, and he only wanted the facts. I introduced myself using one of the best techniques I know for getting places with control freaks: I kept it short, simple, and to the point. I asked to arrange a meeting to discuss the possibility of working together. He promptly let me know that the only reason he was meeting with me was because my client had highly recommended me. "Great," I said, and we set up the meeting.

When I got to the meeting he was there with his right-hand man, Jim. I sat down and went right into business after very brief introductions. Well, you should have seen this guy. He had so much energy he was literally bouncing in his seat. His colleague, Jim, was as calm and cool as a camel in the desert.

I began to talk about the training and consulting projects I was doing with my other client. Bob was as fidgety as a caterpillar picked up by a 2-year-old. I could tell I was boring him to tears, so I changed tactics: I asked questions about his business success and what he wanted for his business. This got his attention, and he talked about how he'd grown the business since he took it over, and about his vision and ability to get his team to work hard and produce.

Note to all of us: Control freaks love to talk about their own successes, how they did it, and how they outpace their competition.

While Bob talked, I took notes. I noticed him sit up a little taller, and then Jim started to chime in. Bob and Jim were already doing things really well within their company and, unless I added something relevant or timely, neither of them was going to see value in working with me. So I told them the story of winning over the CFO of the client who referred me, and Bob's face just lit up. He responded with a true control freak statement: "Well, if you can win Tim over, then you deserve to be in front of my guys."

I love how control freaks don't waste time and keep me on my toes so that I am relevant and timely, and not blowing smoke.

I want to digress here and say that of course not ALL control freaks are fun to be around. Some control freaks have learned to become funky control freaks, and then there are freaky control freaks who still need to work on letting go of being a power freak and focus on behaviors that are effective, not destructive.

Let's face it: Being called a control freak is probably not what every leader aspires to, but I hope that after reading this book you will be encouraged and inspired to look at the positive aspects of control freaks.

In Chapter One I introduced you to the overt, covert, and alert control freak with the overt and covert behaviors being characteristics of a freaky control freak, whereas a funky control freak is alert, aware, and a positive user of control. In Chapter Two I talked about focusing on the strengths of being a positive control freak.

Here, let's go into a little further depth and description of a freaky control freak. (Refer to the chart on page 58.)

A freaky control freak is downright scary. We do not want to practice these thoughts and behaviors, or we will create situations where people will avoid us, become passive-aggressive, with us, or sabotage us.

Many of us have had experiences with freaky control freaks. These are the types of people who help us choose to get another job or get transferred to another department.

When I worked in finance I had a boss whose name was Hal. It should have been Hell. He was that bad.

Thoughts	Behaviors
I am superior to others.	Has a tendency to micromanage.
No one does it as well as I.	Does it instead of letting others do.
Am I the only one who knows this?	Takes over with condescension.
What's wrong with him/her?	Acts bossy and overbearing.
It's not perfect.	Nitpicks and harshly criticizes.
How many times do I have to tell him/her?	Embarrasses in front of others.
I will withhold information to maintain control.	Bullies.

Hal was the type of boss who withheld information and then berated his employees in front of everyone when any of us made a mistake. If we stood up to him or called him on not providing us with the information we needed, he would go into a rage and claim that "good help is hard to find." Hal was the classic example of a freaky control freak. These people are bullies who use passive-aggressive manipulative tactics to get what they want. For those of you needing a refresher about what constitutes passive-aggressive behavior let me remind you:

Passive-aggressive people:

→ Say one thing to your face and another behind your back.

→ Look you in the eye and say they are telling the truth, although later you find out they lied.

→ Manipulate people with false promises and false hope.

→ Use closed body language and closed communication. They do not let anyone in.

→ Want to look good. They revel in making others look bad so they can look better.

→ Suffer from low self-esteem so they try to inflate their results to win favor from authority figures.

→ Will say "nothing," if you ask them what is wrong, but later in the day or week they blow a gasket.

→ Control the office and department in a negative way because no one really knows what to expect from them.

→ Like to instill fear or bully others so they can feel temporarily more powerful.

How to Deal With the Freaky

Very few methods work when dealing with a freaky control freak, but the methods that do work require tremendous confidence, direct communication, and a willingness to hold the freaky control freak accountable for the behavior. When I'd finally had enough of Hell—er, Hal—I confronted him with a list of all of the situations in which I felt I had been set up to fail. (I also contacted Human Resources before I met with him. This way they knew that I was dealing with my boss directly, but were aware of what I planned to cover. If he denied or tried to manipulate the situation I would have our discussion topics on record.)

To prepare for our meeting I wrote down specific situations and examples, and had photocopied the memos involved. (These were the days before saved e-mails.) I knew that by confronting Hal I risked even greater wrath, but I also knew that not confronting him was going to make my life a continued living hell. So what did I have to lose?

I used every assertive technique I knew. I started the meeting by saying that I was having difficulty in my job and that I needed his support to do a better job for him. Immediately he launched into how wonderful he was at his job and how he didn't understand people on his team. He accused the team of being lazy and noncreative, and lacking in initiative. (For the record, in my previous performance review [before working with Hal] I had been rated outstanding, so lazy and lacking in initiative I was not.) *Whenever a freaky control freak focuses on a negative criticism and continues to repeat it the assertive technique to keep you on track is to calmly repeat the facts and focus on the future outcome you would like to achieve.* For example, "I disagree with your comment that you feel the team is lacking in initiative and that they are lazy. This is a generalization, when in fact we achieved the objectives for this month and are prepared for the next month's launch, and I strongly believe our team is on track."

I then listed the situations and examples where I felt he could have provided greater support, information, and follow-up. I brought out the memos and all the supporting documentation to state my case. He looked at my list and at my documentation, and turned bright red. It took all my courage to stay put and stick through the meeting while he became very angry and defensive. I then reiterated my previous successes and my previous performance reviews, and pointed out that perhaps he and I were suffering from personality differences, and that was why we weren't getting the results he wanted.

I asked him to sit with me for one hour each week to review my work and to answer questions so I had all of the information I needed to do my job. I also told him that I responded well to positive reinforcement and recognition. That type of behavior worked better with me than getting angry at or embarrassing me.

I finished the meeting by stating that I really liked my job, but didn't enjoy working in the department, and that I wanted to make it work so we could all succeed. He agreed to my request for the weekly planning meetings and shifted his approach to me completely.

Everyone in the department was shocked that he was being so reasonable with me but not with anyone else. I ended up lasting another six months before I was headhunted away by an insurance company that offered me double my salary, more holidays, and more freedom on the job. When I took the job offer, Hal was personally offended but gave me the greatest gift ever by saying, "You'll be back. And when you come back you will be crawling back." In my mind I said, "Hell will freeze over before I ever come back," and the rest is history. His parting shot was one of the best gifts a freaky control freak could ever give me.

Note to self: When confronting a funky control freak it is not a neat and tidy experience, and can often result in a parting of ways.

Funky Control Freaks

What we do want to do is shift our thoughts and behaviors so that we are funky control freaks. Funky control freaks have the thoughts and behaviors shown in the chart on page 62.

Working for a funky control freak is pure joy. Nothing is more rewarding than working for someone who has clear vision and clear purpose, and who gives clear direction. A funky control freak leader has high confidence, high self-worth, and high level abilities developed over time. Who doesn't want to follow someone such as this?

Thoughts	Behaviors
I am equal to others.	Educates and enlightens.
Everyone has individual abilities.	Adapts to individual personalities and styles.
Have I communicated what I know so that others can succeed?	Provides information so that others have what they need to perform well.
What can I learn from him/her?	Discusses different approaches to getting the job done.
It will never be perfect. I accept close to perfection.	
If I have to keep telling him/her something, how can I use a different approach to get different results?	Comes up with creative ways to communicate.

Assertive communication is the most common method of interaction for a funky control freak. Because he/she has a healthy self-regard, he/she is able to treat others with tremendous respect and value. Here is a refresher in assertive communication:

Assertive people:
- Speak the truth in a way that others can hear.
- Are willing to give feedback that is helpful and allows others to grow.
- Say what they mean and mean what they say.
- Are direct and to the point.

→ Have no hidden agenda.

→ Are open and forthcoming.

→ Are generous with their knowledge.

→ Revel in watching other people grow.

→ Are not threatened by other people out-performing them.

→ Follow through on promises they make.

→ Have clear vision and knowledge of their strengths and weaknesses.

→ Are willing to hear feedback from others to grow and learn.

→ Realize they don't have all the answers. They are willing to find out what they need to know.

→ Inspire others through their directness, honesty, and no-nonsense approach.

→ Create and build trust easily with others.

→ Honor confidences and want to build people up.

Funky Inspiration

I have had the good fortune to work with a few funky control freak leaders who have shaped my own leadership style and abilities. When I got headhunted away from the banking industry my new boss was a powerhouse: smart, intuitive, and in control. I learned a lot from her. Even though she was highly controlling in that she demanded high performance she also rewarded it, so everyone on her team performed to very high levels. It was under her leadership that the private insurance company I worked for out-performed the government agency that held the monopoly on high-ratio insurance for the housing market.

Donna had a way of giving feedback that made you feel good, even when the feedback wasn't positive. I will never forget when she called me in to her office and began to talk to me about the value of quiet confidence. I was in my mid-20s at that time, very ambitious and very vocal about my successes. Donna told me in her direct yet sensitive way that I did not need to go around telling everyone about my wins: my results spoke volumes. She explained that quiet confidence is when you know you are performing at a high level. You do not need to brag, talk about, or bring attention to your results. This was a valuable lesson for me so early in my career, because it caused me to shift how I operated. I believe it was that feedback that helped me get promoted so rapidly and to move on to better things after I left the insurance company.

Funky control freaks know when to let their good people go on to better things.

When I worked for another high-powered female leader named Linda at a credit union I again received invaluable feedback and support to reach higher. I'd been hired by the credit union to head up its new mortgage program. Linda had never done a mortgage program before, so she wasn't sure what to expect in sales volume or dollars booked. A gentleman named Richard and I booked $10 million in mortgages in 10 months in the late 1980s. The credit union could not support this much lending on its deposit base, so in essence Richard and I worked ourselves out of a job.

I was offered an immediate position as a branch manager at the age of 29, which was flattering, but I had already been there and done that when I was with the bank. Linda sat me down for a heart-to-heart about what I really wanted to do and where my talents lie. Linda wanted to me to stay on as a branch manager, but she knew I would be bored in a year. Instead she coached me to follow my dream of starting my own business, being my own boss, and controlling my destiny.

Even though Linda was losing a top performer, she looked beyond her immediate needs and instead looked at the bigger picture of my future. To this day I am grateful that she gave me the gentle push to pursue my passion.

Funky control freaks have a cause, a mission, and a desire to control for their own good and the good of the people around them.

Funky Solutions for Workplace Challenges

Funky control freaks are leaders who have learned to become balanced in their control of power, communication, and behavior. Freaky control freaks are power freaks in that their need to control far overrides their need for autonomy or shared power with others. The funky control freak is best equipped for the challenges in today's work environment.

The varied challenges facing today's workplace include cultural differences, performance challenges, attracting good people, keeping good people, generational differences, and personality differences (which will be discussed in Chapter Five).

Funky control freak leaders find creative ways to meet and overcome such challenges, whereas freaky control freaks just clamp down.

A Funky Solution to Cultural Differences

I know a funky control freak leader who headed up the human resource division of a large healthcare company in California. Her company's diverse culture included a large number of Spanish-speaking, English-speaking, and French-speaking employees. Ellen is a funky control freak in that she provided training opportunities for all of her employees, consistently giving her employees every chance to learn and grow, so that they could perform their jobs to the highest level.

Ellen is a funky control freak who knows that specific skills training in areas such as cultural diversity, communication, customer care, and teamwork allow individuals to increase their knowledge, and ultimately their increased skill sets, resulting in increased performance and employee morale.

Ellen realizes that training is a necessity and that, as a leader, if she does not provide the training opportunities, then it is unfair to expect her employees to perform at the high level she expected.

Funky control freak leaders provide training even if it means that the employees who received the training might take what they learned and work elsewhere. They see training as a necessary investment.

A freaky control freak leader believes that providing training is a wasted expense. A funky control freak leader recognizes training as an investment in the organization's people.

Ellen came up with a creative solution that allowed the diverse cultures within her organization to communicate better and with more effectiveness. She convinced the company to purchase electronic translators for employees who had difficulty communicating with the other languages in the workplace. These translators could scan a word or a sentence in any language and translate it into the primary language of the person using the device. The results of this creative solution were increased performance among the employees, happier customers, and greater teamwork among the culturally diverse employee base. The bridging of the communication gap created greater understanding so that interaction among employees and between employees and the customers improved dramatically.

Ellen took it one step further and provided training in cultural awareness for each of the cultures represented in her company. By focusing on cultural differences as a positive Ellen was able to turn this supposed challenge into a major creative win for the company. Presently Care 1st Health is one of the top-performing care groups in California.

"So she left you. Maybe it wasn't your fault. Sometimes circumstances are beyond your lack of self-control.

A Funky Solution to Generational Differences

Generational differences aren't new at work. It's just that technology has created bigger gaps than we have seen in a while.

The addition of Gen Xers and Gen Yers to organizations means that we are seeing distinct differences in worldviews, values, and work ethic. Baby Boomers (approximately ages 47 to 64) grew up with the idea that you had to work hard to get ahead, earn the right, and pay your dues. Gen Yers believes that life is easy: Just watch reality TV and you will see regular people hitting the big time. Baby Boomers are the parents of Gen Xers and Gen Yers, and have proven to them that they don't have to work hard—because their parents have handed them everything they could possibly want. Many Baby Boomers had to work hard for success, but Gen Xers and Gen Yers believe that work comes second to having a life.

Some Baby Boomers believe you work, work, work, and then you retire or die. Who has it right?

A funky control freak leader knows that there's gold in generational differences at work. Many Baby Boomers have long-term on-the-job training and have historical knowledge. They understand the rationale behind why things are done the way they are done. Gen Xers and Gen Yers question or challenge the way things have been done because they have been raised to be creative thinkers and to use technology to alleviate workload. Many clashes among the generations occur when Baby Boomers do not want to change how it's been done and the Gen Xer or Gen Yer has a creative solution to get it done more easily.

The gold that the funky control freak knows is there is the generational knowledge that can be brought to focus on business results. For example, a story a few years ago in *USA Today* talked about a cosmetics company that used generational knowledge to produce a creative manufacturing solution. Much of the work this cosmetic company did was to make cosmetics by machine and human labor. The challenge was that the labor was assembly-line labor, so every time Bonne Bell hired young people, they would get bored and would eventually leave. The CEO did some research on demographic hiring and advertised the jobs to the 65 and older age group. The result? Bonne Bell attracted post-retirement employees who were thrilled to work and feel needed again. They were loyal and didn't mind the tedious nature of the work. In fact, the CEO commented that because the Veteran/Traditionalist generation (65 and older, loyal, task-oriented) had outgrown the need to resort to behaviors typically exhibited by a younger workforce, there was surprisingly little gossip or backstabbing on the shop floor. This was not discrimination. It was targeted hiring for specific work that would appeal to the demographic of the Veteran/Traditionalist.

Funky Solutions to Attract and Keep Good People

Funky control freak leaders have honed their skills on looking for the right people, hiring the right people, and building control mechanisms that keep the good people.

The leader of a HVAC company based in Portland, Oregon, recognized the perfect profile of the company's ideal employee based on the work it does, the type of employee who has been successful with the company, and the type of workplace environment that would appeal to its ideal employee. In a management retreat the owner identified that the company's ideal hiring candidate was a young man in his mid-20s who liked to hunt and fish.

What does that have to do with air conditioning and heating, you might ask? Well, if we recognize that employees in their mid-20s would be Gen Xers we realize that the generational motto is "Have a life first and work second." So this company, Roth Heating, knew that its top guys were avid hunters and fishermen. It began to use that as part of its recruitment strategy: setting up hiring booths at local hunting and fishing shows, posting job openings in hunting and fishing stores, and putting ads in hunting and fishing magazines. Brilliant? You bet. The company enjoys a constant inflow of prime candidates and the owner, Kory, knows without a control freak doubt that this method of attraction is both creative and right on target.

Is it controlling to do personality assessments when hiring? Yes, and it is funky, too! Funky control freak leaders realize that they can use personality assessments as a valuable hiring tool to determine if the potential employee would fit the culture, the job, and the scope of growth planned for the company. A VP of sales with whom I have worked is employed by a multi-million-dollar construction firm, and he swears by personality assessments. He has a 95 percent success rate in hiring successful sales professionals. The assessments were customized based on the personality traits of his top-performing sales professionals and also on the company environment. Kim states that the only time he made a bad hire was the one time he did not use the personality assessment tool.

Why should a funky control freak be in total control of attracting, hiring, and keeping good people?

A 2006 Right Management Consultants survey found that 68 percent of respondents believe bad hires and promotions lead to lower overall company morale, 66 percent believe they lower productivity, 45 percent say that they cause lost customers, 54 percent say bad hires/promotions produce higher training costs, and 51 percent believe bad hires results in higher overall recruiting costs.

The same survey found that the cost of turnover is approximately twice an employee's salary in recruiting, training, and severance costs.

A 2005 survey conducted by Merrill Lynch found that 25 percent of companies are ready for a mass exodus of employees, but 31 percent haven't thought about it.

Funky control freak leaders also know that they need to have major control mechanisms in place to keep good people. Good people are attracted to company success and brand in the marketplace; they want to be proud of who they work for. In addition, they want to be assured that they will receive ongoing training, support, and coaching.

A 2005 study by Towers Perrin Global produced the following statistics about retaining talent.

Primary reasons employees stay at companies and are engaged include:

1. Manager understands what motivates them.
2. Challenging work.
3. Career advancement.
4. Manager's visibility, honesty, and consistency.
5. Company shows interest in the employee.

(Towers Perrin Global workplace study, executive report 2005)

Perhaps surprisingly, compensation and benefits are not often the reason people leave. Typically management styles, work environment, and direct supervisors have more to do with their decision.

A Sirota Survey Intelligence report in 2006 found that employees who feel that their managers do not respect them are three times more likely to leave their employer in the next two years than those who feel respected.

Resulting from the 1,400 CIOs surveyed by Robert Half Technology in 2005, the following measures have been put into place to retain employees: 63 percent are providing additional training opportunities, 47 percent are allowing employees flex schedules, and 41 percent are increasing base compensation.

The point is that today employees are looking for—begging for—leaders who are funky control freaks. They want a leader with vision and clarity, who provides direction and training, and who is supportive and respectful of his/her employees. What are you doing to develop your funky control freak?

Chapter Four will help you set up your control panel for ultimate power as a funky control freak.

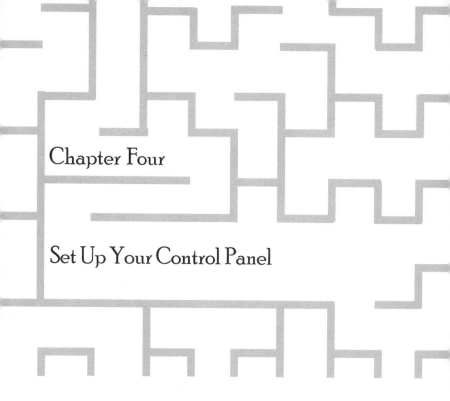

Chapter Four

Set Up Your Control Panel

I'm sorry—if you were right, I'd agree with you.

—Robin Williams

There are two things I ask as a consultant when I am hired to assess an organization: What systems are in place that supports the results you want to create within this company? and, What communication methods do you use to ensure everyone within the organization understands the organizations mission, goals, and expected outcomes?

Every organization needs its control panel of systems and communication mechanisms, and every leader needs to have a personal control panel to guide his/her actions. The control panel introduced in this chapter consists of structures and systems to ensure success. For example, the control panel for a leader struggling with employee performance issues might include a system for ensuring employees' issues are prevented or minimized, and specifically what to do when employee issues arise. Other systems in the control panel might include: managing up (managing those who have seniority over an employee, such as a boss or senior executive), setting employee expectations, standardizing performance reviews, evaluating recognition and rewards, plus much more.

The Personal Control Panel

All of us want to have a sense of control over ourselves, our environment, and our teams. The goal is to ensure that we are focused on the positive aspects of control so that we can create positive results. Let's look firstly at ourselves from a psychological standpoint, and then we can get into understanding others at a deeper level. When it comes to control there are negative drivers of behavior and there are positive drivers of behavior. The negative drivers almost always drain us of energy, as well as those around us. When we focus on the positive drivers we gain energy, and so do those around us. Let's look at the personal control panel.

Personal Control Panel	
Thoughts The Thought Energy Scale	**Behaviors** Communication
Actions Follow-Through	**Outcomes** Positive Work Environment

In the personal control panel there are four areas that we want to positively control: thoughts, behaviors, actions, and outcomes. You may argue that we cannot control outcomes; however, if all of the previous three elements are focused on positive control we can almost with certainty guarantee a positive outcome. Let's start with the thought aspect of our personal control panel.

You of course know that what we think about is what we attract. *The Secret* phenomenon has certainly made that concept mainstream since its DVD release and subsequent book release. There are aspects of *The Secret* that I agree with and one of them is the following excerpt:

> You have a choice right now. Do you want to believe that it's just the luck of the draw and bad things can happen to you at any time? Do you want to believe that you can be in the wrong place at the wrong time? That you have no control over circumstances?
>
> Or do you want to believe and know that your life experience is in your hands and that only all good can come into your life because that is the way you think? You have a choice, and whatever you choose to think will become your life experience.

Think about the application of this from a leadership perspective. The energy you show up with at work is contagious. If you show up at work feeling down, negative, and with no energy then that is the energy that you are spreading around. On the other hand, if you show up for work engaged, inspired, and excited about the challenges, then that too is contagious, and everyone will respond to your example.

Thoughts

Thoughts are the foundation of energy. Let me prove it. Right now I want you to hunch your shoulders, look down at the ground, and say with as much conviction as you can muster, " I feel fantastic." How did that feel? Not so good, did it?

You didn't believe it because your body language did not match the words. Let's try this again. This time stand up or sit up tall with your shoulders back and head held high, and throw your arms over your head and say out loud, "I feel fantastic!" I can guarantee that if you actually did this you felt much more energized by the second go-around. Try this at work and see what everyone else does around you. It's good for some fun.

So let's look at the thought energy scale and see how our thoughts either contribute to positive energy or create negative energy.

The Thought Energy Scale	
Positive Energy	**Negative Energy**
Love.	Boredom.
Appreciation.	Overwhelmed.
Empowerment.	Worry.
Passion.	Doubt.
Enthusiasm.	Blame.
Optimism.	Anger.
Hopefulness.	Fear.

You can see by just looking at the scale how your energy adjusts to the words. When reading the words associated with negative energy, you can feel your own energy level become depleted. When you read the words associated with the positive energy, you can actually feel your energy level go up.

In your personal control panel the goal is to focus your thoughts on the upper range of the scale because that is where the positive actions and behaviors come from. You cannot be in the upper range of the thought energy scale and behave negatively. It is impossible. Don't believe me? Try cutting someone off in traffic deliberately while singing joyously along to one of your all-time favorite tunes. If you can do this then you need further help!

Love is at the highest energy point, and you might think you are paid to work, not love; I would disagree. When we love what we do, love the challenges, love the diversity of people who work with us, and love being alive, we have at our fingertips the highest level of power and control possible. Unfortunately many of us operate at the lower levels of thought energy and we are completely unaware of our thoughts while we are stuck in those thought patterns.

Appreciation is a very high form of thought energy because we are operating based on an attitude of gratitude. When we appreciate our work, appreciate the people we work with, appreciate the opportunities we are given, and appreciate even the smallest of teachings that others are giving us we are operating on higher thought energy. This was put to the test for me while in the midst of writing this book. I had a seemingly innocent encounter that required me to go to the appreciate thought—meaning having thoughts of appreciation for people, events, and situations (as opposed to thoughts of frustration, anger, and so forth). I wrote the following in my blog (at *www.cherylcran.com*) on April 4, 2007:

> Have you ever noticed that when you need to know how things are going in your life you just need to check in with what's happening around you?
>
> Last Sunday I was minding my own business at the grocery store and all of a sudden a

renegade shopper veered in front of me and was ready to cut me off at the produce stand! I managed to give her eye contact and at the very last moment she decided to let me proceed ahead. It was the battle of two shopping carts. Then under her breath the woman said, "You're welcome."

Interesting, fascinating, and cause for pondering. I found myself wanting to react and say something to her but I caught myself and instead proceeded to mind my own business while squeezing the lemons. I did think about this encounter throughout the rest of my shopping and realized that what the shopper was challenging me to do was to simply say thank you.

I am guessing that in her life she rarely gets anyone to give her credit, to make way for her, or to simply say thank you. Her under-the-breath comment was really her venting her frustration, not at me particularly, but at the world in general who just was not responding to her desires.

I found this all very fascinating because I often tell my audiences that someone else's bad day is rarely about us personally and it is usually about other things they have going on. This encounter simply validated this for me and tested me to see how I would react to her projection.

The synergistic part of this encounter was that I had affirmed the day before that I was going to pay more attention for opportunities to be grateful. Well, she certainly put an opportunity right in front of me to think about saying thank you. The reason I didn't say thank you to her in the moment was because I felt I was in the right of way, and no thank you was needed. From her perspective though, she went OUT of her way to make way for me and so I owed her a thank you.

ᴳ᙮ᴚ

Every day we have small moments to choose how we will behave in our interactions. When I translate this to a leadership lesson it boils down to watching carefully how others behave around us, because there are hidden messages in every interaction we have. As a leader, if I am having an "off" day, and I react to others letting me down I need to look at where I myself might be letting the team down, or even myself down.

In my CD and DVD *The Illuminated Leader* I cover the importance of being hyper-aware of what others are reflecting back to us and then use the reflections to learn and grow.

Bottom line: an unknown grocery store shopper caused me stop and think to say thank you.

In 2005, the University of Virginia's Rob Cross and his colleagues asked people in three different organizational "networks" (strategy consultants, engineers, and statisticians) to rate each of their coworkers on this question: When you typically interact with this person, how does it affect your energy level? Cross and his colleagues found that being an energizer was one of the strongest drivers for positive performance evaluations. If we are spending time on the negative energy thought scale we are likely hindering our career.

In our quest to shift from being a freaky control freak to a positive funky control freak, it is important to see the power of words in helping us to make this shift. In the book *The Power Vs. Force,* author David Hawkins lists a number of words that can be more powerful than forceful. Our goal as funky control freaks is to realize the power of power words and the negative outcomes of forceful words. Here are a few examples from the extensive list in Hawkins's book:

Power	Force
Accepting	Rejecting
Admitting	Denying
Agreeable	Condescending
Allowing	Controlling
Authoritative	Dogmatic
Choosing to	Having to
Democratic	Dictatorial
Diplomatic	Deceptive
Encouraging	Promoting
Excellent	Adequate
Experienced	Cynical
Flexible	Rigid
Optimistic	Pessimistic
Powerful	Forceful
Privileged	Entitled

Notice the change in your energy level when you read each power word versus its forceful counterpart: When you read the word *praising* you feel uplifted, and then when you read the word *flattering* you feel a little manipulated.

> *We possess such immense resources of power*
> *that pessimism is a laughable absurdity.*
>
> —Colin Wilson

Behaviors

If thoughts and words are the basis of our energy, then our behaviors are the next step in creating positive control. If you are thinking thoughts that are based on fear, your behaviors will be negative and will result in negative outcomes for both yourself and others. Many of us do not even know that our thoughts are based on negative energy thoughts, and the first step is to recognize where we are on the thought scale. For example if I am in a situation at work where I made a huge mistake and I am afraid to admit it was my fault, then I am in a fear-based thought. That fear thought then creates behaviors that I will use in order to save myself from other fears, such as fear of looking stupid, fear of losing my job, fear of someone else discovering that I messed up—and on it goes. This is the root of CYA (cover your ass) behavior in the workplace. CYA is also the cause of much heartache and nontruthful work environments. From a corporate standpoint the more employees who operate from a place of fear, the more loss in productivity, profit, and results. A Towers Perrin Global Workforce Study from 2005 found that the primary reason employees stay at companies and are engaged include: (1) manager understands what motivates them; (2) challenging work; (3) career advancement; (4) visibility, honesty, and consistency of their manager; and (5) interest in employee. The leadership implication here is that honesty is of the higher energy, and fear-based leadership is at the lower energy and does affect employee engagement and retention.

The best leaders are those who have learned to get rid of fear-based behavior and instead focus on empowerment, passion, and optimism, all of higher energy levels. This reminds me of a boss who exemplifies being completely secure in her talents and therefore could behave in ways that were consistent with higher energy thoughts. Gina worked for a major international bank. She was promoted quickly in her 20s and went on to become a human resources executive in her early 30s. Many wondered how she got promoted so rapidly. When I asked a senior executive that very question, he replied, "Gina does not waste time focusing on what can't be done and why. She instead focuses on where we can improve on processes and she inspires others to want to work hard for her."

I had formerly worked with an employee of Gina's, Lisa, and one day she and I had lunch. I asked her how it was going and she practically glowed with joy about working with Gina. I asked Lisa what it was about Gina that made her such a great leader. Lisa went on to tell me a story about an opportunity to write an article for a major industry magazine concerning the people management strategies of the bank. The opportunity was given to Gina as the executive of human resources. Gina was fully capable of writing the article, and it seemed appropriate that she do so, but Gina was a much bigger thinker, and she offered the opportunity to Lisa, who was a manager in the department.

Now, you might be thinking that Gina was just clever at delegating, and that would be true because every great leader knows that you have to delegate the good stuff as well as the bad. However Gina did something much bigger: She demonstrated that she had complete trust in Lisa to write the article, she was willing to let Lisa get the credit and recognition, AND she created a deeper sense of loyalty from Lisa. Had Gina been someone who operated from fear or competition she would have controlled the need to write the article and she would not have wanted someone else to get the glory.

Think of the behaviors that would follow the positive thought energy list. If your thoughts are based on love, appreciation, empowerment, passion, enthusiasm, optimism, and hopefulness, your behaviors will be gracious, inclusive, considerate, and of high energy. A thought based on negative thought energy creates behaviors of jealousy, negative competition, withholding information, manipulation, coercion, and even sabotage.

On the personal control panel you can see that thoughts and behaviors go hand-in-hand when it comes to being a funky positive control freak.

Actions

Actions are the follow-through to the previous items of thoughts and behaviors. Positive thought creates positive behaviors, which in turn create positive actions. It is actions that speak louder than words. Many employees will leave an organization if they consistently see that the leadership is not walking their talk.

Negative actions have huge consequences. In a 2002 study of workplace aggression and bullying in the U.S. Department of Veterans Affairs, nearly 5,000 employees were surveyed about exposure to 60 "negative workplace actions." Thirty-six percent reported "persistent hostility" from coworkers and supervisors, which meant "experiencing at least one aggressive behavior at least weekly for a period of a year." Nearly 20 percent of employees in the same sample reported being bothered "moderately" to "a great deal" by abusive and aggressive behaviors, including yelling, temper tantrums, put-downs, glaring, exclusion, nasty gossip, and (on relatively rare occasions) "pushing, shoving, biting, kicking, and other assaults."

This is an extreme example of negative actions, but you can see how they are all based on an environment of fear, insecurity, and the negative thought energy scale.

Progress is being made in many industries that used to rely on hierarchal justifications for negative actions. A client I have worked with as a consultant over an 18-month period is a great example of following through on actions that will contribute to overall positive results. As an organization, it invested time and money in providing its leaders with training on all aspects of strong leadership, including training on the various components of strong leadership, but also putting their money where its mouth is and providing individual one-on-one coaching with each of its leaders in order to provide them with the full array of tools to perform their jobs. The leaders who were not willing to work within the positive control parameters were quickly dealt with. The company's hiring criteria is that it will not hire jerks.

Focusing on positive actions creates further positive outcomes.

Outcomes

The fourth component in the personal control panel is outcomes. When our thoughts are focused on the positive energy scale, our behaviors are aligned with those positive thoughts, and we are consistent with positive actions we can guarantee that positive outcomes will follow. When we are clear about the outcomes we would like to create, we can actually work backwards and learn from past experience as well as look at what thoughts, behaviors, and actions we would need in order to produce a new outcome. Jerry Seinfeld did just this before he went on to *Seinfeld* fame. After a bad experience on the sitcom *Benson*, Seinfeld vowed never to do another sitcom until he had more creative control. In 1989, that control was granted, as he partnered up

Cornered
by Mike Baldwin

12-12 © 2006 Mike Baldwin / Dist. by Universal Press Syndicate www.cornered.com
cornered@comic.com

"That's it, I quit. I don't know how anyone can
stand working under you."

with fellow stand-up Larry David to create the *Seinfeld
Chronicles* (which eventually became just *Seinfeld*). The show
was just about Jerry's life as a stand-up comic, dealing with
the little things of modern life. The show developed into a
huge hit. Seinfeld ended the show in 1998 while still on top of
the ratings and critical praise. Jerry Seinfeld knew what he
didn't want and focused his energy on a different outcome.

An executive I coached recently was very clear on what she didn't want, but was struggling with focusing on outcomes she did want. Sara knew that she did not want to continue having to check up on her department managers to see if they were doing the job the way they were supposed to. She also knew she didn't want to keep feeling negative about their abilities. When I pushed her to envision a new and different outcome she couldn't do it. Often we are able to focus on what we don't want while struggling to create what we do want without a little support from an outside source. In working with Sara, I had her envision her ideal workplace in which each individual behaved fully accountable. I asked her the following questions: *What would the energy level be of the office if everyone was fully accountable for their department?* and *What would a typical day look like if everyone was engaged in their work?*

Then we went deeper: *What types of words would everyone be using?* and *What would everyone be doing?*

Sara's answers to these questions were revealing and helped us go to outcome-based leadership. The answers to the questions revealed that the workplace would look very different than it did. For instance, when asked about the energy level, Sara answered that it would be a high energy environment and everyone would be focused on creative solutions as well as taking personal action to make the solutions work. Sara answered that on an ideal day, she would come in to the office and everyone would be smiling, be enjoying themselves, and be eager to interact with each other. The types of words they would be using would be *let's do it, let's see what we can do with this, I will get back to you once I have more information, I will do that, I can do that for you, we will get back to you by tomorrow morning,* and so on. The words used were all active, action-oriented, and accountable. There is always high energy that goes along with positive future-focused action language.

With regard to the question asking what everyone would be doing, Sara saw people talking with each other and then moving on to tasks, and she saw people on their phones being friendly and efficient. She saw focus on projects and communication to all parties affected. When we finished this visioning exercise Sara's energy level had gone up considerably. That was the first step to have Sara create in her thoughts what she did want. From there we worked together for a few months to elevate the behaviors, including how she communicated as well as her actions such as how she set up systems in the workplace so that everyone could do their jobs to the highest level possible. Outcome-based leadership is a system for positively controlling the aspects that you do have direct control over. You have full control over your own thoughts, behaviors, actions, and ultimately the positive outcomes.

The Organizational Control Panel

Once each of the leaders within an organization takes responsibility and operates from his/her own personal control panel we have a greater chance of positively affecting the overall health and success of the organization. Every organization needs its control panel and communication mechanisms. The organizations that have great success are those that have focus on areas of importance and development to their growth.

Many top-performing organizations use a balanced scorecard method as their guiding strategy. Typically there are four components that make up the scorecard:

1. People.
2. Quality.
3. Market Leader.
4. Profitable Growth.

These are broad segments to measure outcomes. However, within the people segment would be human resources, training, recruitment, retention, and engagement. Within the quality segment would be product, knowledge, delivery, client satisfaction, and client retention. In the market leader segment would be innovation, research, competitive awareness, humanitarian outreach, and environmental impact. Profitable growth, of course, would include profits, measurement of profits created by employees, measurement of profits of client retention, and year-by-year comparisons.

In each of these segments the key is the communication of the company control panel to each leader and then subsequent communication to each employee within the organization. Organizations typically stall in growth when they take the time to develop a new strategic plan but do not communicate it with clarity to all levels within the organization. This often results in upper management becoming frustrated that the front line does not know the direction the company is going, even though upper management may have thought they communicated it clearly at the outset.

This is where negative control can become rampant within the organization because the management goes into negative thoughts, such as *We have told them this a hundred times,* or *What's wrong with these people?* Or worse, the leadership begins to micromanage, or takes over because they feel fearful or frustrated at the lack of understanding from their employees. The fear of the leader may be simply that he/she doesn't want his/her team to look as though it doesn't get it, or the leader is overly controlling in a negative way and simply steps over his/her team in order to get the job done. The negative fall out from this type of leadership is massive.

KPMG consistently wins the international employer of choice award. KPMG has a strong commitment to ensure that everyone follows a balanced scorecard. There are systems in place that ensure everyone provides constant tracking and progress reports. The leaders are accountable to the balanced scorecard goals. When a leader does not meet the criteria set out by KPMG it results in not so much a disciplinary process, but rather a coaching opportunity to provide the leader with the tools and techniques needed for them to succeed. Positive control within an organization is based on providing the structure, the tools, and the resources so that everyone can succeed. Positive outcome management from an organizational standpoint can occur when strategies are developed, revisited, communicated, and followed up on for progress.

Renaissance Development, a client I have worked with extensively, is a great example of an organization that took the balanced scorecard to heart. Randy, the CEO, and Tim, the CFO, have a strategy consultant, a people consultant, and a customer consultant. They meet with their strategy consultant quarterly, and on an annual basis the entire leadership team works on the annual strategy. The strategy is then communicated to the entire company through a company-wide meeting. In that meeting both Randy and Tim remain very accessible and open to all questions, and no questions are considered stupid or unnecessary.

After the annual meeting they sit down with each leader of each department and set in place departmental goals that directly relate to the strategy. Then each leader takes his/her goals back to his/her teams and holds a team meeting to communicate everyone's roles in the overall strategy. They also communicate the markers of success that will be looked at along the way. The company meets again as a large group six months after the initial strategy to review its progress. In the meantime each leader is sitting down and coaching each of their employees on their individual goals around the team goals and the company's overall strategy. Again at the end of the year the entire company meets and reviews their goals and what they achieved, and they publicly recognize all the teams that met their goals and targets, and contributed to the company success.

Renaissance Development also puts its money where its mouth is and rewards the results with bonuses. As its people consultant, I work with the executives and the leaders to ensure that all people practices are in alignment with recruiting the best, retaining the top performers, and dealing with those who need further coaching and support in order to improve their performance. I meet with the company quarterly to verify that the quarterly coaching and reviews have been completed, provide training on areas of leadership, coach each leader individually, and confirm that each leader is interacting with the other leaders in a way that supports the overall company goals according to the strategic plan. The company's customer consultant meets with the company quarterly, reviews the policies, and makes sure they are the right ones in place to match the overall strategic plan.

You can see that this company invests tremendous amounts of resources to guarantee that each area of its balanced scorecard gets the same time and attention to ensure that all areas of the organization remain a focus. Many organizations can focus on one area, but then suffer greatly in areas such as profits because they did not look after their people or their customers.

An organizational control panel will look different based on industry, product, or size of the company, but in essence there are many similarities to the process in ensuring positive outcomes as an organization year after year.

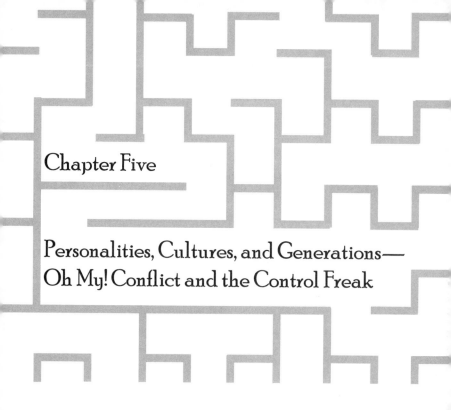

Chapter Five

Personalities, Cultures, and Generations— Oh My! Conflict and the Control Freak

Pick battles big enough to matter, small enough
to win.

—Jonathan Kozol

Have you ever had someone see you do something and then, without your invitation, immediately step in, take over, and make loud sighing noises as if to indicate your massive incompetence?

What would be your response to behavior this type of behavior? Would you like it?

A consulting client of mine had a leader who just didn't trust anyone to do the job the way he did. Mike was well intentioned, but he literally could not let go or let others do the jobs they were supposed to do as part of their job function.

One incident that stands out is when Mike asked his employee to prepare a report that could be used to determine costs of supplies, payments to vendors, and outstanding payables. Mike did not give any further direction or instruction other than stating what it was he wanted as an end result. This management technique can work if you have a full autonomous employee who understands the way you think and if you, as the manager, have provided full training and expectations previously.

In this particular case Mike's employee Rob was unsure of what Mike wanted, but was too passive to speak up and ask questions. Rob's reluctance to speak up was directly related to Mike's leadership style, which was to berate or make his employees feel bad when they did not succeed at a task he had asked them to complete. You can see where this is heading. Rob completed the report but did not check in with Mike to see if he was on the right track, and Mike, as the leader, did not set up checkpoints to review Rob's progress, so the end result was a report that was unsatisfactory. Mike then began to mark up the report with red ink, and handed it back to Rob saying it needed to be fixed. How do you think both Mike and Rob felt with this interaction?

I know that Mike was frustrated and angry, and made the statement that many leaders make: *How many times do I have to tell him/her?* Rob, on the other hand, felt that he did not give the report his best efforts because he said to himself, "What's the point? Mike will just change it and do it himself anyway."

Can you see the endless cycle with this exchange? Have you ever heard the anonymous quotation, "The definition of insanity is saying or doing the same thing over and over again expecting new and different results"?

Mike and Rob ended up having what I call unspoken conflict, which means they both experienced negative feelings about this cycle, but neither spoke of it or worked to resolve it so that it didn't happen in the future.

I was working with Mike as an outsourced coach hired by the executive to help all of the management team with their leadership skills. I sat down with Mike, and we reviewed his style of delegation and how it worked or didn't work. I asked Mike to explain why he was frustrated with his team. Mike went on to talk about how he was raised with the motto "if you want something done right, do it yourself," and he also had an inner belief that no one was as committed as he was to high-quality work. These beliefs and judgments were keeping Mike from leading at his highest possible potential. As long as Mike operated from these beliefs he would continue to create push back from his employees and he would never create an empowered group of employees who produced high-quality work. In the six months that I worked with Mike we focused on clarifying his personality style, his base beliefs and how they contributed to his behaviors, and how to communicate and lead in a way that was inspiring and, in the end, less stressful. We were able to transform Mike's negative control freak tendencies into high-level leadership control skill that shifted his department's success radically.

Now when Mike delegates he clearly defines at the outset what his expected outcome is before he communicates it. Then, when he does communicate it to his employee, he asks the employee to write down the steps he suggests they take to complete the project. Mike also establishes check-in points on a time line so that he and the employee can review what has been done and catch any potential hiccups to the end result. The biggest success factor is that Mike now celebrates with his employee when they do complete the task, and if there are areas that could have been done better Mike turns those into coaching opportunities to guide and help the employee for next time.

Control freak behaviors can contribute to higher levels of conflict. No one likes to be pushed, and negative control freak tendencies always create push back from others.

Funky control freaks can be masters at controlling conflict situations to work in their favor and in the favor of all involved. A number of issues create conflict. One of the major ones is personality. Why do certain people tick us off? Why do we just seem to click with others?

After all is said and done, usually more is said than done.

—Anonymous

Personalities

Many of us may have done many personality assessments, such as Myers-Briggs, DISC, or What's Your Color. However, I still find that many leaders are not fully using their awareness of personality differences to their full advantage.

In my book *Say What You Mean—Mean What You Say,* I developed what I call the 4 D's. The 4 D's stand for:

→ Driver.

→ Dancer.

→ Deflector.

→ Detailer.

My system is a simplified version of personality for the sole purpose of understanding ourselves first and then using personality knowledge to understand those with whom we interact.

Take a few moments to answer the following questions to help determine which "D" is predominant, and in what order your "D"s are in.

When completing the following questionnaire please circle only one response per statement. I am sure you will feel that you could answer more than one, and you might feel that it depends on the scenario as to how you might respond. For the purpose of this assessment simply choose one response with your first reaction.

Personality Assessment Questionnaire

When I am feeling good I express myself with the following behavior:

- A. I high-five others; I talk about why I am feeling good.
- B. I laugh and joke with others.
- C. I tell one person why I am feeling good.
- D. I do not express myself when I feel good.

When I have lots of work to do I tend to:

- A. Head to the office and keep my nose to the grindstone.
- B. Procrastinate slightly by talking to someone first.
- C. Get quite stressed and worry about what others will think if I let them down.
- D. Spend time analyzing what needs to be done.

When I am in a group situation such as the boardroom I typically:

- A. Take charge; ask lots of questions; express loudly.
- B. Crack jokes; bring levity and sometimes sarcasm.
- C. Sit beside someone familiar; stay quiet.
- D. Take notes; think deeply about what is said; say very little.

When I am stressed I will:

- A. Become abrupt and impatient.
- B. Use sarcasm and sometimes blame others.
- C. Become sick; worry about getting it all done.
- D. Internalize my stress; no one needs to see how I feel.

My office or desk looks like:

- A. Stacks of paper piled up; diplomas and trophies displayed.
- B. Paper is spread out, but I know where everything is.

    C. Flowers on the desk; pictures of the kids, grandkids, and pets.

    D. Everything is in its place; labels on most things.

My body posture is often:

    A. Stand tall; shoulders back; walk in a hurry.

    B. Open; smile a lot; may touch your arm when I talk.

    C. Passive; avoid eye contact; may play with a pen or other distraction.

    D. Stand tall; closed arms, crossed; and deliberate movements.

When I speak I:

    A. Talk quickly and loudly; do not ask a lot of questions.

    B. Like to create levity; have a lilt to my voice

    C. Use a lot of ums and ahs; get nervous.

    D. Think before I speak and use deliberate moderation.

When given praise I prefer:

    A. Show me the money!

    B. Praise me loudly in front of my peers, please.

    C. A handwritten note would be fine.

    D. Specific examples of what I did that warrant the praise.

A weakness for me would be:

    A. Impatience.

    B. Disorganization.

    C. Indecisiveness.

    D. Perfectionism.

How others can help me is by:

    A. Saving me time.

    B. Saving me effort.

    C. Saving me from conflict.

    D. Saving face.

My fear is:
- A. Being hustled.
- B. Rejection.
- C. Sudden change.
- D. Criticism.

My need is:
- A. Control.
- B. Approval.
- C. Friendships.
- D. Thoroughness.

To win favor with me, do your tasks:
- A. Rapidly.
- B. Dynamically.
- C. Amiably.
- D. Precisely.

I am motivated by:
- A. Winning.
- B. The chase.
- C. Involvement.
- D. The process.

I am irritated by:
- A. Indecision.
- B. Routine.
- C. Insensitivity.
- D. Unpredictability.

My strength is:
- A. Leadership.
- B. Persuasion.
- C. Listening.
- D. Planning.

Scoring: If you answered mostly A's you fall into the Driver quadrant of the chart on page 99. If you answered mostly B's you fall into the Dancer quadrant, if you answered mostly C's you fall into the Deflector quadrant, and if you answered mostly D's you fall into the Detailer quadrant.

If you found yourself with an equal number of two letters then that simply means that you have equal amounts of two styles. We all have all four styles within us to varying degrees. The point is to see where our predominant styles rest. Once you have determined your predominant style take a look at the chart and let's prove whether or not your predominant style is what came out of the assessment.

Take a look at the chart and put the number four in the quadrant that you think least describes you.

Now put an arrow from the styles that are opposite to each other. For example, the Driver is opposite to the Deflector and the Dancer is opposite to the Detailer.

Typically 95 percent of the time your primary style or number-one style is the one that is opposite to the style that is least like us. If this is not true for you it is likely that you have two styles that are so closely aligned it was difficult to discern your true style that is least like you. So now that you know your number-one style and your number-four style, you get to choose your number-two style and of course the remaining style would be your number three.

So now you should have an order of the styles for you personally. Using me as an example, my order of styles is:

1. Dancer.
2. Driver.
3. Deflector.
4. Detailer.

Driver—Do It and Do It Now	Dancer—Do It and Have Fun
Moves/talks fast.	Moves/talks fast.
Fast decisions.	Likes to socialize.
No small talk.	Smiles a lot/tells jokes.
Business first.	Great starters—difficulty finishing.
No time for niceties.	Likes to gossip.
Results-oriented.	Wants to be recognized loudly.
Show them the money.	Take them for lunch or coffee.
Help them save time.	Help them look good.

Detailer—Do It and Do It Right	Deflector—Can Everyone Get Along?
Moves/talks methodically.	Measures what they say.
Well-thought-out decisions.	Procrastinate decisions.
Reserved and pensive.	Friendly and uses a lot of words.
Perfectionists.	Cares what people think of them.
Needs all the facts and proof.	Doesn't want to hurt others' feelings.
Likes research and writing.	Likes to be given choices.
Uses words such as *thought through, researched,* and *took the time to go over.*	Show interest in them and show concern for them.
Takes time to be thorough and understand their need for detail.	Reassure them and helps them make a decision for less stress.

I have done almost every personality assessment out there, and the results are always the same. People often ask me if we change as we age and the answer is of course. However, most of us will still have our predominant styles in the same order. We will have adapted ourselves, though, to be more balanced in each of the quadrants. The overall goal is that, as funky control freak leaders, we see the value in developing all skills sets within each style and most importantly that we learn to adapt to the differing styles of those around us.

A leader who does not see the value in adapting to other personality styles runs the risk of continued struggle and more instances of conflict.

You can see that the styles most likely to get into conflict would be those that are opposite to each other, but conflict can also arise for those with the same styles. A client of mine has two strong drivers as both her CEO and the CFO, and they can get into major disagreements, especially because each of the secondary styles are opposite to each other. (The CEO's secondary style is Dancer, and the CFO's secondary style is Detailer.) When two Drivers get into conflict it is the battle of the egos, and one of them has got to be willing to give in. In working with both of them I have helped them realize that their conflict is more to do with them both wanting the same end result. This realization has helped them to get over their need to "win" the argument and instead focus on solutions to create the desired outcome.

Generations

This is an interesting time for the workplace regarding the generational gap that exists today. There have always been generation gaps, but the one between a Baby Boomer and a Traditionalist did not seem so stark as the current gap between Gen Xers and Yers and the Baby Boomers.

Generation Yers even have their own language!

> LOL (laugh out loud).
>
> CUL8er (see you later).
>
> PAW (parents are watching).
>
> MOS (mom over shoulder).
>
> 2B (to be).
>
> 2B4U2 (too bad for you too).
>
> 4COL (for crying out loud).
>
> ? U@ (where you at?).
>
> BCNU (be seeing you).
>
> BUKT (but you knew that).
>
> BIBI (bye bye).
>
> CTA (call to action).
>
> MYL (mind your language).

The best inside language we Boomers can come up with is pig Latin, ow-nay at-whay I-ay am-ay aying-say? (Seriously, if you want to decipher your teenager's Gen Y talk, go to *netlingo.com* and find out what they are really saying.)

When hiring this generation, Baby Boomer and Veteran/ Traditionalist bosses have to leave their egos at the door, as this is the multi-tasking generation, who will IM, text, and listen all at the same time. Generation gaps can lead to workplace conflict and dysfunction.

Funky control freak leaders today need to be psychologists. We need to know the personality styles of the people with whom we interact, we need to understand cultural differences, AND we need to understand the psyche's of the different generations.

The effects of generational values on the workplace are far-reaching, and the workplace will be shifting dramatically in the next few years.

We leaders need to be psychological and flexible.

Let's take a look at each of the generations and the age ranges that make up each of them.

Veterans	1922 to 1943
Baby Boomers	1943 to 1960
Generation X	1960 to 1980
Generation Y	1980 and later

Veterans

This is the most loyal generation age range. These employees are post-war, loyal, respectful of authority, task-oriented, and nontechnical.

This is the generation that worked for one company until they retired. They were loyal, and their employer was loyal, too. That is why veteran workers get very upset when their companies downsize or lay off, because the veteran feels loyalty is the utmost of values.

Veterans are frugal, do not believe in debt, and do not understand the massive consumption of material goods by the Boomers, Gen Xers, and Gen Yers.

This venerable generation has lots to offer the workforce and, for specific industries, is a goldmine of potential. Veterans are home and are looking for work. Well-trained Veterans provide several desired skills that employers are continually searching for, including:

→ Leadership.

→ Responsibility.

→ı Mission-critical skills.

→ı A "can-do" attitude.

→ı On time, all the time.

→ı Transferable skills.

Many Veterans are looking for a chance to be productive employees within their community. Veterans have lots to teach us about loyalty and hard work and they want to be in the know technologically. Let's give them some love.

Baby Boomers

Our motto is work, work, work, and then you die.

Seriously, we made different decisions than our parents due to growing up with frugality, not having anything, and rigid rules. Boomers are the largest segment of the population. We decided we would follow the Veteran pattern of loyalty, but then the economics changed and companies began to lay off, restructure, and downsize in increasing ways.

How many of you Boomers reading this have been restructured, downsized, outsized, you name it?

Picture this: You are in your late 20s, you have worked for a bank for 10 years since you left high school, and you get headhunted away to a mortgage insurance company. They offer you $10,000 more per year with more vacation time and more freedom. You jump! Your colleagues say, "What are you, nuts? What about your pension?"

You are 28 years old and you say, "Pension????" and you go to the insurance company.

You love your job, you love your boss, you love your coworkers—it is wonderful! Then they come to you two years later and announce that they are laying off 50 percent of the workforce across the country. They ask you to stay BUT you have to manage the continuing downsize. You try to stay for a few months but can't sleep, and finally tender your resignation.

Wait—it gets better! You find a new job at a financial group as a mortgage development manager and your target is 10 million for the year. You do it in 10 months and they come to you and say, "You have oversold the mortgage portfolio. You no longer have a job, as we do not have the assets to support the volume of lending."

Yes, ladies and gentleman, I stand here as a Boomer who became jaded at the uncertainty of the work environment. The good news is that I decided I wanted to turn my ability to make money for others into a business, and it led me to be the self-employed person I am today.

The implications of a changing work environment, specifically for the Boomers, are that they want entrepreneurial environments with the entrepreneurial perks: flexible work times and schedules, interesting work, and recognition in the form of time off and money.

More Boomers today are becoming entrepreneurs, consultants, and contract workers in order to create this for themselves. What this means to employers is a shift in the traditional models of work and a more creative approach to employee management.

I predict that in the next five to 10 years Boomers will be largely a contract-based workforce, especially those who have already taken pension income from a long-term employer. This sets a precedent for the Gen X and Y because they want to live first and work second.

Generation X and Generation Y

The most important value for the Y generation is friends and family. There is a renaissance in the Gen X and Y to be close to family. That's why most of our kids aren't leaving home until 26—it's sad but true. Because we have made it too darn comfy and FUN. My kids want to hang with us because they think we are cool. We love this, but almost certainly did not have the same relationship with our Veteran parents in most cases.

So what does this mean to us as leaders? It means we need to understand our employees from a generational standpoint in order to both recruit and retain highly talented people. We need to use our knowledge of generations to strategically hire for values and skills that match the jobs we are asking them to do.

From a retention standpoint we need to understand the individual motivators for engagement. For example, a Gen Yer wants above all the ability to have flexibility, which is why many will end up as entrepreneurs or want to work for companies that allow them true entrepreneurial opportunities, which includes rewards to match effort.

This also means a focus on providing training that bridges the gap between current values and skills of each generation to well-rounded skills that can bridge all of the gaps, especially for leaders.

Just recently I was brought on as a consultant to a very successful and dynamic staffing firm. It is number one in the country, and its challenge is getting its Gen X and Gen Y leaders up to speed so that the company can grow to the next level and so that the owners can free up some of their time. This is a young company. (What I mean is that the oldest employee is 40 years old. The average age of its leaders is early 30s—Gen Xers.) I believe one of the main factors for this company's success is its ability to attract high-performing talent at a young age, groom them, and train them. There is a huge amount of loyalty from its staff because the owners hired for personality and culture fit, and were committed to providing as much training as was needed to help each new hire succeed. We often generalize that Gen Xers and Gen Yers are less committed, but I have found that, if they are in a culture that values individuality, provides training, and has ongoing recognition, these two generations thrive.

Lastly, the opportunity for employers means being willing to see different points of views, be less likely to judge them, and instead work to understand them.

Who are we asking to do the changing?

In order to manage generations without conflict we need to understand their values, match the work we give them to their strengths, and respect their unique perspectives and the creativity they bring to the workplace.

"And if I don't see a turnaround soon, I'll be forced to use my outdoor voice."

Whatever your thoughts may be of the younger generations I personally hold out great hope and positive expectation for Generation Y. They are humanitarian, global, and focused on the greater good for all. There was an inspirational story a few years ago about a 16-year-old who was sitting in a Wendy's restaurant. He was a science buff in school and was fascinated with science as it related to benefiting humans. As he was sitting in Wendy's he watched a hearing-impaired person come into the restaurant with his interpreter. They walked up to the counter, and the hearing-impaired individual began to use sign language to order his lunch. The interpreter then spoke the order to the order-taker. The 16-year-old who watched this entire scenario play out thought to himself, "What if we could come up with a way to make hearing-impaired individuals more independent?" The teen went home and devised a glove that goes over the main signing hand, and as the hearing-impaired individual uses sign language it is translated onto a Palm Pilot–like device and can be translated into different languages! This generation is so innovative and entrepreneurial—I swear they will help us to come up with solutions to our environmental concerns.

We need to make a real effort to learn from this generation and to take the time to even learn some of their language. (Remember the list on page 101?)

(To find additional reading on the generations go to my Website (*www.cherylcran.com*), where you can also order my e-book, *The 5 Ways to Lead the Generations*.)

Cultures

As our workplace becomes more and more multicultural we need to be educated about and aware of the different cultural attitudes. We are becoming more and more global in our work, and this is creating new challenges as it relates to language differences, cultural values differences, and work style differences.

In some industries they (the leaders) are focusing their recruiting efforts on specific traits different cultures bring with them. The home-building industry in both the United States and Canada has been suffering a shortage of skilled workers for a few years and is having to come up with creative solutions to this dilemma. An example is a Hawaii-based organization that is focusing its recruiting efforts on specific demographics, such as European immigrants in their early 30s with a Driver personality. The leaders of this organization recognize that although the profile of their ideal hire meets the job requirements, there are unique challenges to managing this type of individual. The challenges include different ways of doing things in America, different levels of understanding of the language, and the inherent personality behaviors of Drivers. As a leader the ability to manage with high levels of positive control requires a commitment to understanding language, culture, and personality.

I worked with a high-level production manager for a major construction firm, and he was so committed to getting the most out of his crew, which included a large number of German hires, that he went and took German language classes. In doing this he demonstrated to his team that he cared enough about them to learn their language, and they respected him that much more. Therefore they worked at a higher level. Technology is also coming up with solutions to the language challenge by creating handheld devices that can be spoken into in one language and then translated out loud.

You can see that if a leader did not take positive control of the language scenario he/she would find him/herself very frustrated, irritated, and probably not much of an inspirational leader.

The work ethics of the cultures are very different as well. A friend of mine has a son, Jackson, who is 6 years old and an avid gymnast. He is very talented and dreams of making it to the Olympics one day. His coach has coached many successful gymnasts in his home country of China. The coach is strict, has high expectations, and does not tolerate the display of emotion. For those of us born and raised in North America, most of us do not have the same dedication to a goal as our Asian counterparts. Think about this from a school standpoint: My daughter found when she was in school that the Asian students worked twice as hard, didn't watch much TV, and got top grades. I am not saying that we do not have a strong work ethic; I am saying that from a cultural standpoint our work ethic can be viewed by other cultures as less committed. Luckily for 6-year-old Jackson, he has fantastic parents who helped him to see that his coach's style although different from his local coach's style was different. Jackson was able to make a choice of what he wanted, and he chose to continue to work with the Asian coach.

The cultural implication requires leaders to use tolerance, understanding and appreciation of the differences, and a willingness to learn.

With so much to be aware of and to learn it can be quite daunting to a control freak leader who wants others to see it his/her way, do it his/her way, and give him/her no grief. On the other hand a positive funky control freak can leverage what he/she has control over to create incredible results. We have control over understanding the different personalities of everyone and to adapt ourselves to those around us, we have control over getting to know the different values of the generations and focus our work tasks to meet the strengths of the natural propensities of each of our team members, and we have control over creatively coming up with ways to communicate with the different cultures, appreciate their cultural contributions, and create a dynamic environment that is joyful to be in.

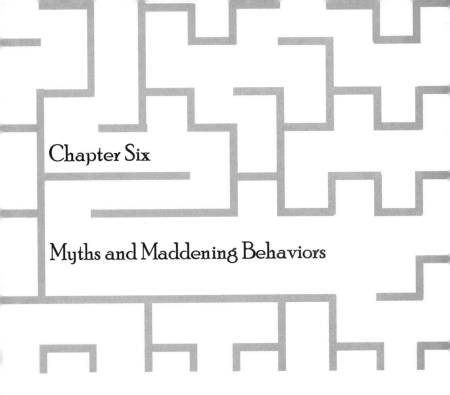

Chapter Six

Myths and Maddening Behaviors

*The great enemy of the truth is very often not
the lie—deliberate, contrived and dishonest, but
the myth, persistent, persuasive, and unrealistic.
Belief in myths allows the comfort of opinion
without the discomfort of thought.*

—John F. Kennedy

Creating myths is a form of negative control over individuals.

Each organization and its individuals generate myths that
are perpetuated based on corporate culture, established patterns, and resistance to change. A funky control freak leader
can bust through his/her personal myths that limit growth and
movement within the organization. A positive funky control
freak leader uses methods for uncovering the myths and then
debunking them. Addressing organizational myths can create
newfound energy, power, and direction for everyone on the

team and in the company. For example, one organization I worked with tried valiantly to get a branch office to adopt a new policy on the use of suppliers. The head office had structured some major cost-savings plans for all branches with specific office suppliers. One branch refused to use the supplier because its branch mythology, originally created by a previous leader, stated that the particular brand it was being told to use wouldn't work with its equipment.

The new positive funky control freak leader in charge of that team went to work on debunking this myth. He demonstrated the actual use of the new supplier's materials in the branch's equipment in a team meeting. When the entire team saw that the equipment would indeed work it adopted the new supplier without any further resistance.

Debunking myths often means someone must physically demonstrate that the myth is untrue. In this case the funky control freak leader took the time to first understand that the team resistance to the supplier wasn't logical, but was very real. Secondly, the leader realized that he needed to take positive action to dispel the myth. By taking the time to address the issues—not dismiss or ignore the issues—and then to demonstrate the positive results of using the new supplier's materials successfully, the leader collapsed any further resistance the team might have to adopting the new supplier.

Where do these myths get created in the first place?

Typically it is either a leader who was a negative control freak and established a myth to help them retain control, or it is a control freak employee who spread the negative myth to the point of integration.

What are some of the myths of your individuals and of your organization?

Myths are the same as negative beliefs that have become firmly entrenched with the organizational culture. It is important to realize that, although you may know the myth is not true, to those who have ingrained it into their belief system it can create negative behaviors, teams, and results. As leaders we need to identify which myths may be circulating and then build a strategy to bust those myths.

Here's a list of some common myths or beliefs that can get established:

→ **Myth #1: Job security.**
The belief that your job will be more secure as long as you're the only one knowledgeable about a certain topic, or if you're the only one capable of doing a particular task.

→ **Myth #2: Gaining personal advantage.**
Holding knowledge for ransom from those not in-the-know and using the old "you scratch my back, I'll scratch yours" bartering system.

→ **Myth #3: Competition and internal rivalries.**
Hoarding knowledge in order to best colleagues.

→ **Myth #4: Knowledge as power.**
The belief that the more you know, the more well-regarded and indispensable you will be.

→ **Myth #5: Fear of nonrecognition.**
Afraid that someone else will take credit for your work.

→ **Myth #6: Fear of accountability.**
Afraid that someone will misuse your knowledge and you will get blamed for it.

→ **Myth #7: Loner attitudes.**
Refusing to actively seek out information from colleagues, preferring to figure things out on your own.

→ **Myth #8: Fear of incompetence.**

Afraid to ask for help for fear of being made to look as though you're not pulling your own weight.

→ **Myth #9: "Wasting" time.**

The idea that "knowledge sharing helps others, not me," and that it will take valuable time out of your own busy schedule with little personal reward.

It's important that you don't allow whatever negative cultural influences that exist within your organization to paint an overly grim and cynical picture of corporate life. In most cases these counterproductive behaviors are the exception, not the norm. Although these behaviors are extremely difficult to predict, there are ways to minimize their impact on your knowledge sharing initiative and even to effect a real positive change within your organization.

This essay (my paraphrase of an essay written by an anonymous Microsoft employee) is an example of cultural mythology:

> We suffer from a phenomenon that I've seen at other companies. I describe this as the "personality cult," wherein one mid-level manager accumulates a handful of loyal "fans" and moves with them from project to project. Typically the manager gets hired into a new group, and (once established) starts bringing in the rest of his/her fan club. Once one of these "cults" is entrenched, everyone else can give up from frustration and transfer to another team, or else wait for the cult to eventually leave (and hope the team survives and isn't immediately invaded by another cult). I've seen as many as three cults

operating simultaneously side-by-side within a single product group. Rarely, a sizeable revolt happens and the team kicks the cult out. Sometimes, the cult disintegrates (usually taking the team with it). Usually, the cult just moves on to the Next Big Thing, losing or gaining a few members at each transfer.

The cult gives the manager the appearance of broad support, and makes the few people who speak out against him/her look like sour grapes unrepresentative of a larger majority. After a string of successes, the manager is nearly invincible.

Fortunately, these managers are unlikely to move further up the ranks, due to the inherent deficiencies in their characters (which are usually visible to upper management and enough to prevent their advancement, but not so severe as to warrant firing them).

These "personality cults" always negatively impact the group eventually (while they're there and/or when they leave), but counter intuitively sometimes these personality cults have a large positive initial effect. Many successful Microsoft products have come into existence only through the actions of such personality cults. Some of these products even survived after the personality cult left for the Next Big Thing.

This story about personality cults can be viewed as either positive or negative, but the fact remains that this mythology has created in at least one employee's mind the idea that unless you are part of the "personality cult" you do not stand much of a chance of success.

Let's look at the myths and beliefs listed previously and address them each individually from two perspectives: first, the impact these mythologies and beliefs can have on the organization, and secondly, how a funky control freak leader can go about busting the myths for greater team and organizational success.

"Your report just tells me what I already know. Good work. I hate surprises."

Myth #1: Job Security

The belief that your job will be more secure as long as you're the only one knowledgeable about a certain topic, or if you're the only one capable of doing a particular task.

A negative or freaky control freak leader often perpetuates this myth. This is control in its ugliest form because it hoards all knowledge and all power over a certain topic or area of expertise. The dangers to the organization of having leaders or employees buy in to this myth or belief is enormous. From a succession planning standpoint, if there are not mechanisms in place to deal with this, then the organization suffers from poor succession planning, lack of team cooperation, and poor public perception.

The executive and leaders of the organization need to do a culture check to see to what extent this particular myth exists within their organization. At the end of this chapter is a checklist that will assist in identifying which myths may be hindering growth of the organization or of individuals within the organization.

I worked with Don, a 34-year-old Generation X executive who has been on the executive team of a very large and successful development company. Don brings youth, vibrancy, and energy to the team, but he also has the belief or mythology that, as long as he keeps all information and knowledge to himself, then he guarantees control over his destiny and his place within the company. I was hired to coach him and to work with him on management skills, as he had had no previous training or experience in leading others. In the initial personality assessment that he completed it was very obvious that he was a strong Driver/Detailer personality, which indicates highly controlling and highly analytical. This meant he got things done and he was accurate, which made him indispensable to the company as well as a dangerous link in the future growth of the company.

I worked with Don over the course of 10 months, and the first six months were not successful. Each time I would point out how his belief that he had to keep all information for himself and that no one else could do what he did was hurting the company. He would nod his head and then go back to his regular behavior.

Finally, on the seventh coaching visit, something clicked for him when he realized that his belief was holding him back from having a life. While he worked hard due to his own insistence of knowing all things and not sharing that knowledge, his colleagues were leaving at a decent hour and not working on weekends. It was the obvious demonstration of what his behavior was creating in others that caused him to shift. Now Don has delegated major projects and areas of expertise to various people within the organization, and he was surprised to find that he felt a whole lot lighter and that his boss was more impressed by his ability to manage others, which meant he had further solidified himself within the executive team.

As leaders we need to coach others to see that job security is certainly not guaranteed to those who hoard or hide information from others. Rather, job security is usually a given to those with high levels of ability to share information, inspire others to higher performance, and contribute results to the team and the company overall.

Myth #2: Gaining Personal Advantage

Holding knowledge for ransom from those not in-the-know and using the old "you scratch my back, I'll scratch yours" bartering system.

Hierarchal systems within organizations are needed for high functioning teams. However, when hierarchy is misused as abuse of power, this can create a fear-based culture. The goal to gain personal advantage is a form of negative control, plain and simple. It gives the hoarder a false sense of security. The organization suffers from this form of control in that the behavior is based on bribery or one-upmanship. It also creates silos or micro-cultures within the organization similar to the theory of the TV show *Survivor*, where anyone who does not play the game of "bartering for information" gets voted off the island or treated poorly because they are not willing to play along. This is exactly the type of behavior that also can contribute to another Enron scenario, where information is secretly held and shared with few who can be trusted, and we all know what happened in the end of that story when some had the courage to bust that myth.

Myth #3: Competition and Internal Rivalries

Hoarding knowledge in order to best colleagues.

A new term has been created to explain the shift away from competition toward competing with cooperation. The term is *coopetition*. The benefit to organizations in shifting from an internal competitive environment to a cooperative is that it works for the greater benefit of the individuals and the organization. Now, some of you reading this that are in sales will be saying, "What are you, nuts?" You may believe that having healthy competition between your sales professionals is a good thing for both them and the company. Well, let's look at this from a broader perspective: If we have internal competition, yes, we may get more sales, but at what cost? The cost is lack of trust between sales team members, lack of creativity due to hoarding of ideas and knowledge, and finally lack of synergy as each person is out for him/herself instead of the company, the team, or even the client. Of course offering commissions and incentives for increased production is a staple of incentive for performance, but the innovative organization rewards and recognizes team results, provides team incentives, and rewards team cooperation and creativity as components of success.

Often when the organizational culture rewards the very things it wishes to create the rewards shift the negative myth or cultural beliefs, and creates an environment of connection, great ideas, and tremendous growth.

Hoarding knowledge to best a coworker ultimately harms the customer and can result in negative customer perceptions on the company brand as a whole. For example, a pharmaceutical group for which I did some consulting work was finding that its clinical study groups were not entering all of the crucial data needed for accurate analysis of the study results. When the group investigated why the data was not being captured, it came down to certain individuals within each group that had the information but chose not to enter it, due to keeping the information for themselves in the event that it was asked for and they could appear "in the know" or invaluable to the group's study. The area team leader had the idea to gather all groups together and discuss the company's goal to dispel myths regarding certain behaviors that could negatively affect team performance. Once the behavior was "outed" with no particular person targeted, and optional behaviors or choices were presented, the groups went back and within one month of data capture all information was now being gathered. This resulted in more accurate results, better team relations, and ultimately successful study results.

Myth #4: Knowledge as Power

The belief that the more you know, the more well-regarded and indispensable you will be.

Many organizations have individuals who believe that, because of their education or the length of time on the job, they are superior to others. Many leaders are afflicted with this belief or mythology, and it can be destructive to the organization overall. Often with individuals who believe they know more than you know behave with arrogance, and are condescending and overly controlling. In this era where we are in an employee's market (in other words, employees hold the upper hand with companies looking to recruit more people) it is important that organizations recognize this belief or myth, and nip this one in the bud through coaching. Better yet, develop a hiring questionnaire that allows you to discover these hidden myths and beliefs in potential hires.

There is no question that people who have earned their degrees have worked hard. However, there are others who are as intelligent and effective, but who may not have the same level of formal education. I often tell my audiences that I have a PhD in life! Seriously, how many of us can honestly say that, given our work experience, life experience, and continuing investment in lifelong learning?

I was conducting a seminar about 10 years ago in Van Nuys, California, on conflict management. Typically the people who come to that seminar have been sent because their company is secretly hoping they will get "fixed." When I started the seminar I said to the group that we would be looking at conflict from a psychological standpoint, and a woman who was sitting front and center stood up. Her face was beet red, and she was shaking with anger. She shouted out loud in front of 75 people, "Do you have a PhD in psychology?" I don't know if you have ever felt that you are in the Twilight Zone, but I stood there, and I swear I heard "nee, nee, nee, nee." Because I was teaching conflict management, I knew that I had to stay calm and not get riled, but she had me sweating. My hands were shaking, and I put them behind my back to stop the shaking while I replied, "No. I do not have a PhD in psychology; however, I do have years of training and certificates, and I am the seminar leader today. I will give you two choices: You can stay, or you can leave." She stayed until the break. For the rest of the morning I would go to one side of the audience and they would all be giving me the thumbs up for support, then I would go to the other side of the room and they would be smiling at me for support. When the break came a fellow who had been sitting at the back of the room came up to me and said, "I work with that person."

That woman's behavior was clearly based on her internal belief that, because she did have a PhD, it made her superior to everyone else, that she had nothing more to learn, and that she could treat others poorly because of that belief. By the way, the fellow who said he worked with her let me know a month later that she was let go from her employer shortly after she attended the seminar. Was she indispensable? I don't think so.

Myth #5: Fear of Nonrecognition

Afraid that someone else will take credit for your work.

This myth can be a leaders Achilles' heel. A freaky control freak leader bases his/her need to control on this myth. He/she does not want to share the glory with his/her team, because if he/she does not take full credit then he/she will not be viewed as THE person the company needs to keep. The challenge to the organization with this behavior is that it creates teams that lack trust of both their leader and their team members. It also lowers morale as employees begin to give up on their efforts, knowing that they won't get the credit they deserve anyway.

When I worked for a major mortgage insurance group about 14 years ago our branch leader suffered from this belief or myth. Bruce was very fearful that the company would not keep him unless he constantly communicated the branch's wins as his own. He would brag about how under his leadership the branch was succeeding and never credited anyone else for the contributions. While I worked there I got frustrated more than once at the obvious lack of regard he had for his managers and ultimately all of the employees. After working with this company for two years it announced that it would be laying off 50 percent of the employees across the country.

Bruce became even more protective of his perceived value to the company and continued to take credit as the go-to person. He asked me to stay on, as he saw me as a valuable asset, and part of the reason was because I had never challenged him on taking all the credit for my team's wins. Although I was flattered that I was asked to stay, I had to leave because I just couldn't stomach the leadership being demonstrated. Leaders who have the courage to give credit where it is due become well-loved leaders.

Remember I said earlier that people don't leave their jobs—they leave their leaders? I went on to work for other leaders who were fantastic at recognizing contribution and sharing good news results with their bosses as well as sharing it with the entire company through internal newsletters, company meetings, and in person.

Myth #6: Fear of Accountability

Afraid that someone will misuse your knowledge and you will get blamed for it.

This is a very real fear that still exists in organizations today, even though the word *accountability* has become a buzzword for our times. As a consultant and a speaker I am often asked by executives who hire me to enforce a message of personal responsibility. Accountability is an interesting thing because it is one thing to ask people to step up and take responsibility, but then the organization has to ensure that it is not punishing or retaliating against those who step up. This would create a mythology within the company culture that, although the company pays lip service to accountability, no one wants to take it because of the potential negative outcomes from upper management.

Recently I was a keynote speaker for a large health group where there were 2,000 attendees. In my preparations I always interview at least five or six attendees as well as talk with the organizing committee. The health group had been going through major change, and one of the key messages the group wanted me to get across was the need to be brave enough to hold crucial conversations within the organization. The health group was heading into a process known as appreciative inquiry, and it required every participant's willingness to be open about issues such as accountability, leadership, and team challenges. I was happy to include the value of crucial conversations in the presentation, but I did mention to the organizing committee that asking people to be brave enough to bust through a fear or myth is one thing, but providing the support and safe environment for employees to do this was a significant factor that had to be taken into consideration. The executive team agreed and has implemented a series of check points and systems to ensure that there will be no retaliation toward anyone who speaks the truth, who takes accountability for a situation, or who "outs" behaviors that are detrimental to the organization overall. The individual leader needs to ensure that he/she communicates regularly to his/her team that accountability is expected, that there will not be punitive action taken, and that those who take positive accountability and action will be recognized and rewarded.

Myth #7: Loner Attitudes

Refusing to actively seek out information from colleagues, preferring to figure things out on your own.

Organizations can unwittingly create a culture of lone rangers or lone wolves. The two personalities that tend toward this behavior are often the Driver or the Detailer. Some corporate cultures actually perpetuate this type of behavior because they want their employees to be solution-oriented. However, loner attitudes can have a major impact on company productivity. Getting information from a colleague, rather than reinventing the wheel, is a big time-saver. Creating a culture of mavericks can also cause past information to get overlooked, which could result in activities that are a waste of time. Of course, we don't want leaders and employees to be overly dependent on others or to not figure things out for themselves. What we do want is to ensure that the mythology of figuring things out on our own doesn't become a hindrance to seeking information from others.

A consulting client of mine has a controller with whom I have done some coaching work over a period of 12 months. The person the company controller hired had come from a completely different industry, but brought years of experience in the financial field. Barry brought fresh ideas and energy to the company, but had a maverick attitude. He wanted to show the chief operating officer that he was good at what he did and that he was a worthy hire. As you can imagine, it was a steep learning curve from his previous industry of a large corporate retailer to home development.

For the first six months Barry really struggled because his desire to be a star without taking the time to figure out the industry caused him great stress and actually backfired. The COO wasn't quite sure about Barry's overall abilities after six months, and I encouraged each of them separately to spend more time with each other to share information. When the coaching was completed Barry realized that in his efforts to impress, he actually caused himself more stress, and learned that he needed to learn more and ask questions of others in order to do a good job for the company.

Myth #8: Fear of Incompetence

Afraid to ask for help for fear of being made to look as though you're not pulling your own weight.

In the previous story Barry also suffered from this fear or myth. Part of the reason for this was that the company culture overall placed a high premium on all of its employees being highly intelligent self-starters. Barry's boss, the COO, is a highly intelligent and critical thinker, so when Barry approached his boss for help he was worried that the work he presented for review would be criticized. Fear of criticism goes along with fear of incompetence, because when we do ask for help we don't want to look stupid, and we secretly hope that what we produce meets with instant approval. Again the organization and its leaders need to ensure that all employees are allowed to ask for help without fear of being viewed negatively. Otherwise performance issues will come up, due to employees hiding their blunders or efforts, and ultimately this affects the company, the team, and the customer.

Myth #9: "Wasting" Time

The idea that "knowledge sharing helps others, not me," and that it will take valuable time out of your own busy schedule with little personal reward.

Oh, boy—this is a big one! Many, many leaders buy into this myth or belief, and it can be devastating to an organization. Companies that encourage knowledge-sharing benefit from greater succession planning and growth planning overall. There are still a number of organizations that have not held their leaders' feet to the fire over this issue. Of course everyone is very busy, and time is a premium these days. Organizational leaders who fail to recognize the danger of this myth could risk the very future of the organization. Stephen Covey made the following statement a well-worn one: "If you fail to plan—you plan to fail." Strategic plans for organizations need to include a strategy for getting information out of the heads of those who hold a lot of knowledge as well as for those who have long time on the job knowledge. This is a crucial component to succession planning.

I have consulted with many companies that failed to recognize the value in getting information out of the heads of the knowledge-keepers and into the heads of those who need to know. The companies that have recognized the value have set up structures for cross-training, information-sharing meetings, and data downloads into company intranets for easy access by team members. Of course the company needs to also dispel the myth and belief that knowledge-sharing is a waste of time and encourage leaders and employees through distinct incentives for those who willingly share knowledge.

A large construction company I worked with about four years ago has offices in Colorado and California as well as Calgary and Toronto. The company had hired me to facilitate its executive retreat on succession planning. It was a two-day session, and the first item on the agenda was to discuss and list the known knowledge-keepers of the organization. This is a very large company, and yet the list of knowledge-keepers was relatively short. This was a visual sign that something was amiss, and the executive at the meeting could not ignore. In fact that year one of the company's top operational executives had suffered a heart attack, and the entire operation was compromised for six months. Luckily it was solid enough to withstand the setback, but many companies today would not be so lucky.

At the end of the two-day retreat we had devised strategies and implementation plans on ensuring that within a one-year time frame the number of knowledge-keepers on the list would triple. An argument against undertaking this type of strategy might be that it is time-consuming, but in the end it is absolutely vital to keeping the organization in business.

What Myths Exist In Your Organization?

Yes	No	
☐	☐	Do we have a number of people who feel entitled?
☐	☐	Do we have people unwilling to share knowledge?
☐	☐	Is there an undercurrent of a lack of trust?
☐	☐	Do some departments have their own set of rules?
☐	☐	Do we have people who are focused on self interests?
☐	☐	Do we have a succession plan in place?
☐	☐	Do we have leaders who fail to recognize others?
☐	☐	Are people afraid to take personal responsibility?

If you answered yes to three or more, then your company has a moderate level of mythology that is affecting business success. If you answered yes to more than five, there are negative myths perpetuated that need to be addressed immediately.

What can you do? First, the organization's executive leaders need to recognize the myths that exist. Second, they need to buy in to the concept of busting these myths, and third, they need to address the myths through a strategy planning session with all leaders within the organization. From there the leaders need to carry forward the company's commitment to shifting the corporate culture away from the ingrained negative myths toward an open and sharing culture where these behaviors are recognized and rewarded.

What can you do as an individual? You can bring the checklist results to the attention of your boss, and request action or take the initiative yourself within your own department to make positive change. Many cultural shifts have occurred due to a high-performing department's initiative and courage to tackle the myths that can harm, not help, business.

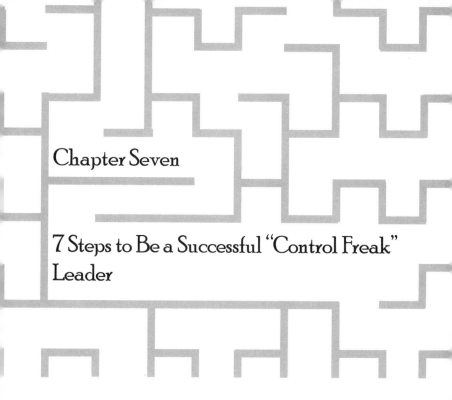

Chapter Seven

7 Steps to Be a Successful "Control Freak" Leader

As long as you're going to be thinking anyway, think big.

—Donald Trump

Brian is a top CEO for a major high-end carpet retailer. The company provides eco-friendly carpet and flooring, and its main clientele consists of interior designers. Brian had taken over for a much-loved leader who retired. Brian was hired from Chicago and brought to the Seattle office, where he was responsible for a staff of 15. I received a phone call from Brian requesting that I facilitate a company retreat.

When I met with him to do a pre-consultation prior to the retreat, I asked him to list his strengths and then his areas for improvement. As a leader Brian felt his skills were to provide direction, strong vision, clear goals, high standards, and results. I asked Brian if he was willing to have his new team evaluate their first impressions of him and if he was willing to address the feedback at the retreat. At first Brian balked, as he felt that asking his team to evaluate him so early in his tenure would diminish his position as leader. I explained that by asking the team for the initial perceptions and then to address them would allow us to leverage the retreat, and the team could see that Brian was willing to grow, learn, and respect the opinions of his team.

At the retreat we covered the elements of managing change, and we had a group discussion about the much-loved leader who had retired. I asked the group what they loved about that leader, and the list included things such as *he cared deeply, he took the time to explain things, he was concerned for their well-being,* and *the customers loved him.* I then told the group that having a loved leader leave was very difficult, and that it was natural to mourn the loss of a leader who was loved. We then discussed the importance of moving forward and adapting to change. I asked the group to list some of the attributes they noticed about Brian in his first three months on the job. The list for Brian included *results-oriented, focused on profits, visionary,* and *disciplined.* It was a very different list than that of the loved leader before him.

I then had Brian address the group, thanking them for their analysis of his leadership, and he made a commitment to earn their trust and love over the next six months. He then went on to tell them more about himself, his leadership style, and the areas that he was willing to work on in order to best support the company and the team. Brian was intelligent enough to know that there is no point in competing with a loved leader who has gone before him. He also realized in our work together that he had to win the team's love, and the first step was to endear himself to the group through feedback and acknowledgement of his style. It was a brave thing to do, and the group responded very well. We followed up the retreat with coaching for each leader, and within six months Brian had doubled the results of the company with his team, and the team had supported him as their leader willingly and with energy.

Only the bravest control freak leaders open themselves up to critical analysis willingly. The high-performing leaders of today have high degrees of positive control freak traits. They also adopt traits based on feedback of peers and employees.

There are seven steps to being a successful positive control freak leader:

1. Self-control: Be aware of self.
2. Reality check: See yourself in reality.
3. Learn and grow: Projection and reflection.
4. Psyche control: Archetypes and you.
5. Use of time control: Conscious personal leadership.
6. Inspiring others through positive control.
7. Success control: Helping others to succeed.

1. Self-Control: Be Aware of Self

First you must learn to control yourself. The rest follows. Blessed is he who knows himself and commands himself, for the world is his and love and happiness and peace walk with him wherever he goes.

—Robert Heinlein

There are three principles of self-awareness:

1. Effective leaders understand their own assumptions about human nature.
2. How you lead is influenced by who you are and the demands of the situation.

3. Expanding your self-awareness, situational awareness, and ability to adapt your leadership style increase your overall range of effectiveness as a leader.

Effective leaders understand their own assumptions about human nature.

Our assumptions about human nature are based on our previous experiences, but also on our own personal viewpoints about people in general. For example, if we grew up in a fairly remote area, we did not travel at all as a child, and our community was mostly one culture, we may have developed a perception that people should only behave the way we became accustomed to. We may be prejudiced against others based on our limited exposure to culture and the world at large. If, as leader, we do not have the awareness of how our environment has shaped us, we can find ourselves in blind spots and can shorten our tenure as a leader within an organization. I mentioned the four different generations in Chapter Five and the awareness we need to have about the viewpoints and values of other generations, personalities, and cultures.

A highly self-aware leader understands his/her biases and why he/she has them. Some positive assumptions about human behavior could be:

→ All humans are inherently good.

→ All humans behave in ways that are sometimes difficult to understand.

→ All humans have other things going on in their lives that may cause them to behave in ways that are unexpected.

→ All humans want to succeed and want to receive praise and recognition.

A self-aware leader who operates from these assumptions will lead from a place of positive assumption about people. This leads us to the next principle of self-awareness.

How you lead is influenced by who you are and the demands of the situation.

A highly evolved leader recognizes through learning and experiences that who he/she is and how he/she views his/her situations will determine his/her behavior when dealing with others. Who you are is determined by your assumptions and how you see yourself in relation to others. For example, in the story about Brian at the beginning of this chapter, Brian is someone who wanted success. Success is one of his guiding principles. He knew that, in order to gain success with his new position and his new team, he needed to adapt to the situation and shift his self-perception in order to achieve the success he wanted.

In Chapter Five we talked about personality differences. Brian is a Driver personality whose main value is to "get it done." The much-loved leader who had left was a Deflector personality whose motto is "why can't everyone get along?" They are directly opposite to each other with regard to style: The Driver is all about results, and the Deflector is all about the people. If how we lead is influenced by who we are, then it stands to reason that Brian was to have an uphill battle in gaining his team's love if he was not willing to shift who he was by adapting some of the thoughts and behaviors of a Deflector personality.

This leads us to the next level of self-awareness, which includes situational awareness.

Expanding your self-awareness, situational awareness, and ability to adapt your leadership style increases your overall range of effectiveness as a leader.

In the example with Brian, he was self-aware enough to know that his main personality style was not going to be well received given the situation he had entered. He recognized that the situation warranted his willingness to adapt his leadership style to increase his overall effectiveness as a leader. You might be asking yourself, *What if the situation were different? How could Brian adapt?* Well if Brian had arrived with the previous leader being highly autocratic, dictatorial, and rigid, he would have still followed the same process of holding a company retreat, conducting an employee survey, and then addressing the strengths the previous leader contributed to the company and how different his approach was going to be moving forward.

The self-aware leader recognizes that each situation requires its own analysis, unique approach, and an inventory of how best to approach the situation for overall success for everyone involved.

2. Reality Check: See Yourself in Reality
Humility is to make a right estimate of oneself.

—Harry Truman

The Office has become a popular show to TV audiences in North America because of the exaggeration of bad boss behavior presented by the main character, Michael, portrayed by Steve Carrell. Any of us who regularly watch this show probably chuckles out loud and covers his/her eyes with horror at some of his bad behavior antics. One of the character traits of Michael as a boss is that he certainly sees himself as the best boss, and he does not have one ounce of seeing himself in reality. In fact the humor of the show is that he constantly ends up coming off as an ass because of his self-inflated sense of self. He also does not have an ounce of humility, which makes him even more unlikable. I can think of one episode in particular when Michael applies for a promotion at his company's head office and, before even going to the interview, assures his team that he is leaving;

he sets it up so that everyone in the office has to compete to win his job once he gets his promotion. The reason it was so funny is because of the arrogance and the stupidity. This guy has no sense of seeing himself in reality and has a very high, self-inflated sense of self. The result is that everyone who works for him is laughing at him constantly. His deepest desire is to be a deeply respected boss, and so he fakes his way through by pretending to know more than he really does, sets up internal competitions for his favor, and wants the prettiest girl in the office to think he's hot. Oh, my gosh!

Leaders may not see themselves the way others see them. Part of the reality-check process is to be willing to ask peers and team members for feedback, insight, and peer reviews in order to have a full picture of how we are perceived. Leaders who do see themselves in reality do not delude themselves into thinking they are the be all, end all, or that they have higher self-importance than anyone else.

A coaching tool that I use with clients and leaders that I work with is something I call the mini 360. The mini 360 is where I provide a list of skills that are needed in order for that individual to perform at his/her highest level possible. The person being coached then rates him/herself using a simple scale of one to 10 (with 10 being highly rated). Then we send that same list of skills to that person's peers, boss, and employees. The responses are anonymous and are e-mailed back directly to my office. A report is then compiled that includes all feedback.

It continually pleases me that, when the results of the mini 360 are delivered to the person being coached, there is tremendous growth, surprise, and a wake-up call. The results can be humbling as we may rate ourselves as a "10" as a communicator, but three people could have rated us as a "4" in communication.

This doesn't make him/her wrong; it simply means that he/she has a specific perception based on how we interact with him/her. This requires us to face the reality of how others see us whether we like what we hear or not. This reality check can be very powerful in shifting our approach to everyone we interact with on a daily basis. I have seen entire departments and companies transform as each person being coached integrates the feedback they received from the mini 360. (In Chapter Eight we explore the full concept of this multi-rater performance feedback mechanism and how it can help you as a leader.)

Leaders who do regular reality checks are definitely positive funky control freaks.

3. Learn and Grow: Projection and Reflection

How many legs does a dog have if you call the
tail a leg? Four. Calling a tail a leg doesn't
make it a leg.

—Abraham Lincoln

Have you ever asked yourself the following question: *How many times do I have to tell him/her?* If you have, then you know the frustration that comes along with that question. If you are asking the question in the first place it is likely that you have been participating in a self-created pattern that will not change until you learn what is being reflected back to you, and then you change your approach.

Definition of insanity: Doing the same thing
over and over again expecting new and different
results.

—Anonymous

Positive control freak leaders have heightened their awareness to such a state that they realize every situation, every encounter, and every interaction is an opportunity to learn, grow, and develop both as a leader and as an individual. A great question to ask when we find ourselves faced with challenges is: *What can I learn from this?* Asking ourselves that question allows us to remain humble and open to internal cues about what to do or to what the possible solution may be.

The two tools of learning and growing are projection and reflection. With projection we want to check ourselves to see if our viewpoint is shaping what we expect to see in others or in specific situations. For example, you may have heard of the story of two women seated beside each other on an airplane. One woman began to eat crackers out of a bag that was right between the two ladies. The other woman was shocked and thought to herself, *How dare she? Those are my crackers!* Nevertheless she continued to get more and more indignant as this woman nonchalantly ate the bag of crackers. She even offered some to the woman. *The nerve!* she thought to herself. Finally in a huff the first woman said, "I hope you enjoyed MY crackers!" The second woman responded in a huff, "Those were MY crackers." The first woman then looked in her bag and there were her crackers.

The moral of the story is that we see what we choose to see and often react before responding. A negative control freak will project on to others what he/she expects and what he/she wants to see, and this can cause major stress and challenge for everyone. In the book *I Can Read You Like a Book* by Gregory Hartley and Maryann Karinch, they further explain projection as follows:

> Projection means you see what you want to see. We project weakness of all kinds onto a person who has any weakness of body. We refuse to believe that a frail looking senior citizen can murder or that someone in a wheelchair could commit a terrorist act. And when we accuse someone like that of a crime, what are we upright, healthy folks likely to feel? Guilt.

In *6 Habits of Highly Effective Bosses,* authors Stephen E. Kohn and Vincent D. O'Connell offer this tool with regard to uncovering a projection:

> Focus on blind spots. Create your own radar warning system! When you are given information that opens an entirely new awareness for you, label it as such: "It uncovered a blind spot for me." Such a label reinforces that, somehow, you had been "blinded" to a certain reality that others had perceived about you. An active relentless effort to seek feedback from others reduces the likelihood that your "blind spots" will persist.

It is a humbling realization that every person with whom we interact is actually reflecting an aspect of ourselves. Carl Jung acknowledged that the very personality trait we found disgusting in another person was really an opportunity for us to take a look at that trait within ourselves. For example, if you work with someone who continually drives you crazy or irritates you it's likely that he/she is modeling a behavior that you either believe you yourself would never do, or he/she is reflecting to you something you may be doing unconsciously. Recently I had a scenario in a group where there was a leader who I found extremely frustrating. I thought he was wishy-washy, nondirect, and lacked follow-through. I knew that if I was reacting this strongly there was something for me to look at on a personal leadership level. For months I found myself getting frustrated by his behavior, and I found out that the very behavior traits I was harshly judging were traits that could be perceived in me by certain people. This is hard to acknowledge but extremely helpful, because it allows us to not become arrogant or self-righteous about our own behavior. No one is beyond reproach. It's important to know too that we don't have to spend a lot of time with the people who we don't have mutual respect for, and that we can manage our interactions with the people who trigger us, so that we choose how and when we interact and at what level.

A positive funky control freak catches his/her projections and takes time to reflect before speaking, before making a decision, or before making changes.

Reflection is a big component of growth. Many leaders, especially control freak leaders, do not give themselves permission to take the time to reflect. When I consult with senior executives and order them to spend at least three hours a week in reflection, I almost always get the same response: *What? I don't have time to be idle.*

So then I suggest that they reflect while doing other mundane tasks such as driving, playing golf, at night in a journal before bed, early in the morning at the office before everyone else gets in, or while exercising. Reflection does not mean sitting still with your eyes closed, although I am an advocate for this form of reflection as well.

Lifelong learning and growing are fundamental to being a highly effective person, let alone a leader. I often say to my audiences that if you think you already know what there is to know, then you might want to look over your shoulder. My personal belief is the day any of us knows it all is the day we are dead. And then what a waste, because we have no way of telling anyone!

4. Psyche Control: Archetypes and You
Everything that irritates us about others can lead us to an understanding of ourselves.

—Carl Jung

Carl Jung was a Swiss psychiatrist, influential thinker, and founder of analytical psychology. He was also the originator of the concept of archetypes and how they shape our personal behaviors as well as the behaviors of others. I could write an entire book on my understanding of archetypes, and there are many resources to further dig into this fascinating concept. For the purpose of this book and to support the control freak leader who wants to be the best leader he/she can possibly be, I feel it is imperative to include the basics of archetypes to help us look at ourselves and deepen our self-awareness as well as provide us with a tool to recognize the archetypes evident in those we interact with.

Archetypes are the basis of personality types. Myers-Briggs, DISC, and most personality assessments are based on the premise of archetypes. Common archetypes are the warrior, the teacher, the mother, the father, the sibling, the child, and so forth. I find it fascinating that in the workplace we all bring our unique archetypes to the table. I myself discovered that I had warrior and teacher archetypes at play in my psyche, but that in identifying with these archetypes I had little patience with the mother or child archetype.

I see many times in an office environment where family roles play out unconsciously among team members. One company I worked for many years ago had a woman named Connie who definitely represented the mother archetype. She took everyone under her wing, brought baked goods in every week, cared about peoples' lives, and gave advice on love and family. When someone's archetype is accepted it can actually help to create an enjoyable work environment. However, when an archetype is overwhelming it can cause conflict and upheaval. Connie's mothering did not sit well with everyone in the office until one day Doug, who exhibited negative behaviors of the sibling archetype (such as backbiting, competitiveness, striving for attention, and downplaying others' accomplishments), got into a major conflict with Connie because she projected her mothering onto him. Neither of them was aware of the archetypes they were engaging, and for me to observe the behavior was quite fascinating. Finally one day the three of us had a discussion that I facilitated. I pointed out to Connie how her behaviors could be perceived as mothering. I also pointed out to Doug how his behaviors could be perceived as sibling rivalry. When I, an outside observer, brought awareness to their individual behaviors of archetypes, they were shocked at how their behaviors were being perceived.

As a leader the more psychological awareness we have of what makes people tick, why people do what they do, and what components make up behavior, the more skills we have to facilitate solutions.

5. Use of Time Control: Conscious Personal Leadership

Gain control of your time and you will gain control of your life.

—John L. Mason

The Blackberry has created monsters of all of us. Really? As a funky control freak I love PDAs. Time control is the key: We all have the same 86,400 seconds per day; it really just depends on what we choose to do with our time. It does seem that there aren't enough hours in the day, that there are too many interruptions, and that we never seem to get through our to-do lists. Blackberries, Treos, and the like are tools that we can CONTROL to help us to be more efficient. When I first got my Blackberry I resisted using it because I had become so used to my Day Timer. I loved my Day Timer—the bulk of it, and the practicality of it. Everything was stored in there, and God help me if I lost it. Eventually I transferred everything to the Blackberry, and I love it. The first thing I disabled was the annoying noise factor of either a beep or a buzz for every e-mail that comes in. The first week I thought I'd kill someone if I heard one more beep. Once I disabled that function I have learned to love the efficiency of this tool.

Positive control freaks have gotten very good at managing their time. Randy Sebastian, the CEO of Renaissance Homes, is a time-management master. This is a CEO who manages to get in two hours a day at the gym, take his daughter to dance, close a deal on 100 acres of land, and attend two or three meetings at the office on a daily basis. How does he do it? He has learned to let go and give up control to his COO, Tim, and his executive team. Randy admits that it took him years to get to where he is now with his team, and he has given them complete autonomy to make decisions that are in the best interest of the company.

As a leader you may not have the luxury to delegate as highly as Randy does, but there are certainly ways you can leverage your time. First of all, if you are an admitted control freak, then it is a given that delegation is hard for you. The proven steps to successful delegation are:

- Clearly define the expectations of the project or task.
- Provide resources and tools to help your employees along the way.
- Check in periodically to see how they are doing.
- Provide guidance and support.
- Congratulate and praise them for doing the job well.

The key to successful delegation is to set up your employees for success. Do not delegate just the crappy jobs or tasks. Make sure you delegate tasks and projects that are in alignment with their skills and talents.

6. Inspiring Others Through Positive Control

Everyone thinks of changing the world, but no one thinks of changing himself.

—Leo Tolstoy

The following excerpt is from the book *The Hands-Off Manager* by Steve Chandler and Duane Black. The authors confirm the benefits of positive control:

> Old school managers keep trying to fix things. They keep trying to fix people.
>
> They go through endless inept exercises to try to find ways to motivate mismatched employees to get them to do what they don't want to do. They try to find ways to make them change themselves into someone they are not. This is a waste of everyone's energy!

Whenever we try to fix anyone, we are controlling. Our goal is not to fix; our goal is to inspire to action. Recently I delivered a keynote on working with the different generations in the workplace. There was time for questions and answers, and one vice president of an eco-friendly textiles firm asked me how she could get her Generation Y employees to stay on task. I asked her if she had "fun time" during the day. The whole audience looked at me aghast. My point in asking the question was that Gen Y cannot be fixed into a Baby Boomer worker mentality. They need to be inspired into it, and they need to understand the whys, the hows, and the rationale behind our request. This may sound exhausting, but it is true. My suggestion was to provide 10 minutes of team fun each day with care to not make it cheesy, stupid, or mundane. (A few examples are playing ping-pong, having a game of charades, and dancing.) Get them to create their definition of fun. Once they know that there is guaranteed to be fun each day you can then get them to focus on task when it is "work" time. Trust me: Younger people today are used to school environments where fun was mixed in with learning, and by segmenting those activities they will have longer periods of focused attention.

Positive control requires creativity and new approaches. We cannot use old-style management habits in this new age of work. Inspire rather than fix, and you will be a positive funky control freak leader.

7. Success Control: Helping Others to Succeed

*It is literally true that you can succeed best
and quickest by helping others to succeed.*

—Napoleon Hill

Peter Legge is the president and CEO of Canada Wide Magazines and a dear friend. I believe one of the most elemental factors in Peter's success as a businessman and as a leader is that he displays full positive control over his thoughts, behaviors, and actions. More importantly, he helps others to succeed. A person who is truly confident in his/her abilities, contributions, and talents knows that the best legacy he/she can leave is to empower others to succeed.

I met Peter when I was working for a credit union about 14 years ago. I was volunteering for a children's charity golf fundraiser, and I was the ninth-tee greeter. I brought a book to read (Izrat Khan's *Mastery*) to read in between foursomes. As each group arrived, I greeted them. In one particular group, one of the gentleman looked at my book and asked me what I was reading. I was embarrassed, because it was not your everyday read. Another gentleman said, "Do you know who this is?" pointing to Peter. I said that I did not and handed the book to Peter. The gentleman beside Peter went on to tell me that Peter was the president of Canada Wide Magazines, and had written numerous books and was a well-known professional speaker.

It was quite synchronistic, because I was working with a career coach to shift my career and to become self-employed. On impulse I asked Peter if I could have lunch with him to ask him questions. He readily agreed and told me to call his assistant, Janice. I did, so the next day and the day after that I had lunch with Peter. In that one hour I took copious notes and left that luncheon undertaking every action Peter suggested I take in order to be a successful entrepreneur. I stayed in touch with Peter, and every six months since that first lunch we have met for either breakfast and lunch. Peter supported me to be a successful businesswoman, author, and speaker, and he has helped countless others, too. He publicly announces that he is no longer available as a mentor because he just becomes too inundated with requests.

When I talk to any of Peter's employees, they always say he is the best boss to work for and that he takes pride in helping all of his employees succeed. The positive outcome of helping others to succeed is that we get the good feeling that comes with that, too. Many leaders feel they just don't have the time to train others or to teach someone to do a project or a task. This is a typical control freak thought, because we want to control our time and what we know, and deep down we are not sure of the return on our investment. Or we ask ourselves WIFM (what's in it for me)?

In Chapter Eight we will dig deeper in to the leadership evaluation tool, the 360-degree performance review process, and discover how it can help us to be the best leader possible.

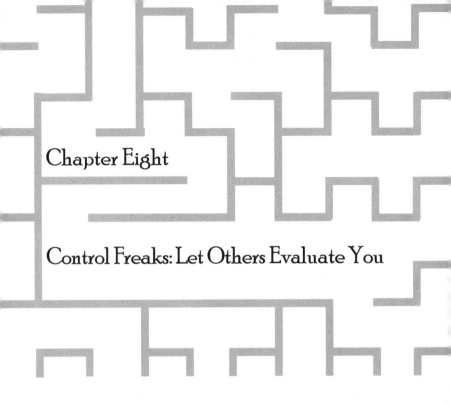

Chapter Eight

Control Freaks: Let Others Evaluate You

*Used artfully, feedback on competencies can be
a priceless tool for self-examination and for
cultivating change and growth. Used poorly it
can be an emotional bludgeon.*

—Daniel Goleman, PhD

Do you enjoy being criticized? If you are a control freak,
the likely answer is no. Let's face it: Most of us would rather be
praised than criticized. Yet I am sure you can think of a time
when well-timed, well-spoken, and well-delivered feedback
helped you to be a better leader.

I shared with you earlier that I have had the great fortune
of having many forms of feedback in my previous corporate
career, but also as a professional speaker and as a consultant.
When I was in banking and insurance I worked for a few bosses

who were fantastic at providing honest feedback. On the other hand, the boss's opinion or review is only one perspective of many with whom we work.

Leadership performance reviews used to be written by the leader's supervisor only. One prevalent attitude in the workplace

"At least with me, when you screw up, you know where you stand."

could be that if the boss is happy, then it didn't matter what anyone else thought of the leader. The shift in collaborative work teams within organizations has caused leaders to be willing to receive multiple performance assessments. One tool that helps leaders to access the perspectives of their work teams and other leaders is through the 360 performance review process. The 360 performance review provides leaders with an excellent overview of what their peers and employees perceive. This multi-faceted approach to performance can be a powerful tool that causes leaders to be fully accountable to the entire team, not just the leaders' immediate superior. There are many formats for the successful implementation of a 360-degree performance assessment within an organization. The 360 review process is one of many ways to commit to being a whole new leader, and we will investigate the choices here in this chapter.

A few factors determine whether a 360-degree process will be successful or not. There are also a variety of ways to prepare and deliver 360 feedbacks for maximum success within the organization, and for the leaders and their employees.

If your organization does not currently have the 360 process in place you could still institute your own mini version of a 360 within your department and as a growth tool for you yourself as a leader.

Some questions to ask yourself prior to implementing a mini 360 or to have your company implement a 360-degree program are:

→ı **Is our organization ready for 360-degree feedback?**
The answer to this question needs to be investigated. There is much value in the preparation for a 360-degree program as there is in the actual set up and implementation of it.

→ı **What is 360-degree feedback?**

The process includes collecting perceptions about a person's behavior and the impact of that behavior from the person's peer, boss, or direct reports. Some 360-degree programs include feedback from suppliers, internal and external customers, and project teams.

→ı **Do we have the resources to set up a 360-degree feedback program?**

The effectiveness of a 360-degree feedback program depends on ensuring that the feedback is directly linked to the integrity of the program. Many organizations set up a project team to evaluate the best format, questions, and delivery systems for maximum results within the company.

→ı **What is our overall goal in setting up a 360-degree feedback program?**

The overall goal needs to be aligned with the corporate mission, vision, and values, as well as the corporate strategy. If one of your main values is that your people be your number-one customer, then the overall goal for the 360 would be to support everyone to be reviewed for personal growth, team value, and company value.

Further questions the organizing team would ask themselves while planning the process would be:

→ı What is the role of senior management and HR in the process?

→ı Do we have the resources to manage the 360 in-house, or do we need to outsource a consultant to facilitate the process?

→ Are we committed to providing staff training based on the outcomes of the 360 reviews?

→ Will we involve customer perceptions in our first go-around of the 360 process?

→ What support will we provide in the form of coaching to follow up on the feedback received for participants?

→ What is the purpose for our company in conducting the 360-degree feedback process?

In a 2006 survey conducted by Lepsinger and Lucia, when participants responded to the question, "Who is the 360-degree feedback system being used in your company?" the results were:

→ For management and organizational development: 58 percent.

→ For performance appraisal: 25 percent.

→ For support strategy implementation and culture change: 20 percent.

→ For team development: 19 percent.

The best outcomes of a successful 360-degree process come when it is used to link employee and leadership development with organizational goals in a format that supports the overall corporate strategy.

When I speak to audiences and ask for a show of hands of those who have participated in a 360-degree performance program, typically about half of each group puts up their hands. When I ask again how many found it to be valuable, only about 25 percent of the room puts up their hands. It is important to point out that, when the 360-degree review process is used as a "search and destroy tool," or to "out the negative types," or to piggyback on employee performance reviews, it can be counterproductive and destructive.

The successes I have seen with organizations that use the 360-degree review process come from those that use the tool for management and organizational development.

When the organization wants to achieve a business strategy and culture change, it identifies the behaviors that are required to support its initiatives. For example, an international games company wanted to shift the company leader's style away from silo leadership, where each department operates as its own entity. In order to determine the leadership behaviors that were needed, the executive spent time preparing for the 360-degree process by holding a leadership strategy session where each leader contributed ideas to ensure that each department's leaders used similar behaviors in order to get department results while meeting the business strategy goals. Once the leadership behaviors were identified they were included in the 360-degree assessments so that any behavior gaps in skill would be easy to see, and coaching to build those skills could be set up. Including the stakeholders in the beginning of the process is a key element in the 360-degree program's success.

The other way to use the 360 for maximum success is to enhance team effectiveness by identifying the gaps in team skill sets. Team effectiveness is crucial to organizational success, and the 360-degree feedback system can be a phenomenal tool in bringing the obvious skill gaps into focus and using that information to increase skill sets individually and for the team. For example, an international textiles wholesaler had a sales team that needed to produce superior results. Each team member operated individually without considering the whole, such as the team or the corporate goals. By using the 360 process the team was able to identify the team behaviors needed and then translate those behaviors into the 360-degree questionnaire. The rating of each behavior for each team member helped to reveal quite quickly and effectively where a team member needed to adapt or be supported in order to contribute at higher levels to the team.

Finally, a successful use of 360-degree reviews is for leadership analysis overall. When a leader is evaluated based on the perceptions of his/her peers, direct reports, and boss, it is a tremendously valuable teaching and training tool. I worked with a business coach when I started my first service business back in 1991. One of the coaching tools he used with me was a mini 360 review. I was to be reviewed on my sales ability, entrepreneurial capacity, and ability to adapt to the uncertainty of self-employment. As part of the coaching process I completed a personality assessment and then had a mini 360 review completed by my peers, my husband, and my coach. What I discovered completely blew me away; some of the behaviors that I thought were strengths were perceived differently by those who worked with me. At the time my husband and I owned this business jointly, and his assessment of my behaviors was quite eye-opening. For instance, although I rated myself as quite proficient at sales, four of my assessors viewed me as too passive. When I investigated this with my coach he pointed out that I was great at closing sales once they were in the funnel, but I was quite lazy with my prospecting. It was fascinating to have this feedback—and highly valuable. The important component of using the 360 for leadership development is to have the person being assessed complete a self-evaluation in order to compare perceptions during the 360 degree meeting where the feedback is delivered face to face.

The Right Reasons to Set Up 360-Degree Feedback

It is very important that you recognize that you are asking people to be honest and the process requires integrity. If they believe that it will be used as a disciplinarian or downsizing tool, you will take away the trust and intent of the process. Rather, 360-degree reviews should be seen as a way for improving performance, offering training, and coaching in order to grow the leaders.

You want to increase loyalty and buy-in to the corporate goals and believe the 360-degree review will assist the employees and the organization in achieving its goals. It is important to communicate from beginning to end about the intent of the process, the goals of the process, and the overall outcomes, actions, and follow-up.

You want to use a tool to help, not as a weapon. Experts recommend not using the 360 as part of the overall performance review system; it is important that 360 is seen as one tool or component of overall performance assessment.

Your organization values open communication and employee empowerment, and you see the assessment process as an empowering tool. If your organization is highly bureaucratic and communication is not valued, then there are other organizational challenges that would prohibit a successful 360-degree program.

The 7 Steps to a Successful Organizational 360-Degree Program

The organizations that have had great success with the 360-degree program have used a process similar to the following to ensure maximum success:

→ **Step 1:** Form a team to investigate a variety of 360 programs and prepare a report back to management on the format that the project team recommends. Choose a test pilot group (preferably senior management).

→| **Step 2:** Once the format is agreed upon hold a company-wide meeting to communicate that the company is undertaking 360-degree reviews and that senior management is going first as part of the test pilot, and openly discuss pros, cons, questions, and concerns.

→| **Step 3:** Each leader is provided with the complete details on how to complete the reviews, how many reviews each employee should complete, and the time lines. Training is provided to the leaders on how to best complete and deliver results.

→| **Step 4:** The project team communicates with the leaders by following up on specific touch points agreed upon in the time line with the leaders.

→| **Step 5:** The employees involved complete the feedback either in an online format, intranet format, or by hand. (This depends on company size, scope of reviews, and so forth.)

→| **Step 6:** Data are compiled and gathered by designated consultant or HR representative, and results are sent to each leader of the person who was evaluated. A follow-up meeting is held with all leaders on how to deliver the reviews.

→| **Step 7:** The results of the 360 reviews are delivered in a one-on-one meeting with specific focus on positive growth and goal-setting. Follow up to the goal setting is established 90 days post–360 review completion.

Senior management should be the in the test pilot group, as this demonstrates the willingness to be open and to use the process as a development tool. One home builder organization I worked with on the 360-degree review process chose to have its top management be the first or test pilots of the 360-degree process because the senior management wanted to show others at different levels that they were open and agreeable to the process. When the employees saw the willingness with which senior management participated, it increased their trust for the process and increased their eagerness to participate.

Set Up Your Own Personal Leadership 360 Review

If your organization is not in the process of implementing a 360-degree review process, there is nothing to stop you from gaining the benefits of receiving feedback from your peers and employees. In fact, you will find yourself gathering fantastic information for your own performance improvement, and your peers and employees will have increased respect for you as a leader as they see your willingness to open to subjective feedback. You can create a very simplified 360 process by listing areas that you feel are relevant to your job and have your evaluators rate you on a scale of one to 10. There are certain steps for success in ensuring you get the most out of the process, and that those involved find it to be a positive exercise.

The self-review could be managed by you from start to finish, but I highly recommend hiring a coach or someone from your HR department to lead the process for you so that you receive only the compiled results.

5 Steps to a Successful Self 360 Review

→ **Step 1:** Communicate to your boss and HR your intentions to set up your own 360 process for your own leadership development.

Advise them as to whether you are doing this through a coach or through HR. Ask for their support and promise to provide them with the results once the process is completed.

→| **Step 2:** The coach or HR professional can use your current performance review ranking criteria to create your list of leadership skills and behaviors that you feel make a good leader and are crucial to the high performance in your specific role. (A sample is provided on page 160 as a starting point.) Communicate to your peers and direct reports the project you are undertaking to better develop yourself as a leader.

→| **Step 3:** Have the forms sent for completion and ensure participants that their comments and review completion are known only by the HR professional or the coach, and that you as the leader will only be receiving the compiled results. Complete your own self-assessment using the same form to compare your perceptions with the others.

→| **Step 4:** Arrange a meeting with the coach or HR professional to go over the results of the mini 360 reviews. Make sure you go in with a calm and open frame of mind, and keep your focus on learning and growing from the experience.

→| **Step 5:** Commit to taking action on the areas that were shown for you to improve. Meet with each contributor individually and thank him/her for the feedback, make the commitment that you are taking the feedback seriously, communicate the action you are taking with the results, and promise to follow up in 30 days to communicate your progress.

Sample Assessment for Mini 360 Review

This is completed by those evaluating you as well as for you to use as a self evaluation tool.

Assessment for Leaders

Please rate yourself on a scale of 1 to 10 with 10 being high in each of the following:

1. _____ overall communication skills

2. _____ ability to handle conflict

3. _____ ability to adapt to change

4. _____ ability to manage multiple priorities

5. _____ ability to not take things personally

6. _____ ability to work together as a team

7. _____ ability to set high goals

8. _____ ability to follow through on commitments

9. _____ ability to lead others

10. _____ ability to take control and have authority

11. _____ ability to see different perspectives

12. _____ ability to manage emotions

13. _____ awareness of how you are perceived by others

14. _____ ability to handle feedback without being defensive

15. _____ ability to sell your opinion or influence others

16. _____ ability to manage stress effectively

17. _____ ability to balance personal time with work time

18. _____ have successful relationships outside of work

19. _____ spend time on outside interests or hobbies

20. _____ ability to ask for support when needed

21. _____ ability to inspire and motivate others

22. _____ ability to stay positive and focused on future solutions

23. _____ ability to communicate vision and turn into accountable action

చి—

I have also included a sample of a 360 questionnaire that could be used for a formal organizational 360-degree process.

360-Degree Evaluation Questionnaire

Management Evaluation Date: _____

Person being reviewed: _____

_____

This is a 360-degree management evaluation questionnaire. Your feedback is valued as a way to support the growth and ability of the person you are evaluating.

Please be supportive in your comments that you provide after each rating.

Specific examples are needed so that the person being evaluated can follow through on changing based on the feedback provided.

Example:

Demonstrates understanding of the overall business goals of the company.

____	0–25% of the time	____	51–75% of the time
____	26–50% of the time	____	76–100% of the time

This person has a very good understanding of the business goals of the company. He/she has a strategic plan for his/her department that is closely aligned with the overall company goals. He/she has ongoing team meetings to share that understanding with the rest of the team.

Please consider these guidelines to make this evaluation most helpful:

What do you appreciate about the person's work style? What do you not appreciate?

What do they specifically do or not do that you would recommend they adjust?

1. ## Business Skills and Experience

    Demonstrates understanding of the overall business goals of the company.

____ 0–25% of the time	____ 51–75% of the time
____ 26–50% of the time	____ 76–100% of the time

    Example:

    _____

    _____

    _____

    _____

    _____

    _____

    Demonstrates the ability to be proactive versus reactive.

____ 0–25% of the time	____ 51–75% of the time
____ 26–50% of the time	____ 76–100% of the time

    Example:

    _____

    _____

    _____

    _____

    _____

    _____

Demonstrates problem-solving abilities.

____ 0–25% of the time   ____ 51–75% of the time

____ 26–50% of the time   ____ 76–100% of the time

Example:

_____

_____

_____

_____

_____

_____

Demonstrates decision-making abilities through analysis and information-gathering.

____ 0–25% of the time   ____ 51–75% of the time

____ 26–50% of the time   ____ 76–100% of the time

Example:

_____

_____

_____

_____

_____

_____

_____

Demonstrates follow-through on commitments made.

____ 0–25% of the time ____ 51–75% of the time

____ 26–50% of the time ____ 76–100% of the time

Example:

_____

_____

_____

_____

_____

_____

2. Professional and Technical Skills

Demonstrates a willingness to continue to learn and to increase knowledge of business.

____ 0–25% of the time ____ 51–75% of the time

____ 26–50% of the time ____ 76–100% of the time

Example:

_____

_____

_____

_____

_____

_____

Demonstrates a complete understanding of his/her job and his/her role in his/her department.

_____ 0–25% of the time   _____ 51–75% of the time

_____ 26–50% of the time   _____ 76–100% of the time

Example:

_____

_____

_____

_____

_____

_____

Demonstrates the ability to manage multiple priorities.

_____ 0–25% of the time   _____ 51–75% of the time

_____ 26–50% of the time   _____ 76–100% of the time

Example:

_____

_____

_____

_____

_____

_____

_____

Demonstrates the ability to prepare in advance for meetings and considers others' time.

____ 0–25% of the time   ____ 51–75% of the time

____ 26–50% of the time   ____ 76–100% of the time

Example:

_____

_____

_____

_____

_____

_____

Understands the technical aspects of his/her job.

____ 0–25% of the time   ____ 51–75% of the time

____ 26–50% of the time   ____ 76–100% of the time

Example:

_____

_____

_____

_____

_____

_____

_____

3. Teamwork

Shows strong team skills, contributes to team success, and understands team roles.

____ 0–25% of the time   ____ 51–75% of the time

____ 26–50% of the time   ____ 76–100% of the time

Example:

_____

_____

_____

_____

_____

_____

Shows respect for everyone within the company and respects other departments.

____ 0–25% of the time   ____ 51–75% of the time

____ 26–50% of the time   ____ 76–100% of the time

Example:

_____

_____

_____

_____

_____

_____

Demonstrates personal leadership by taking accountability and not blaming others.

____ 0–25% of the time ____ 51–75% of the time

____ 26–50% of the time ____ 76–100% of the time

Example:

_____

_____

_____

_____

_____

_____

Is solution-oriented and thinks of solutions before bringing problems to others.

____ 0–25% of the time ____ 51–75% of the time

____ 26–50% of the time ____ 76–100% of the time

Example:

_____

_____

_____

_____

_____

_____

_____

4. Communication

Communicates openly, honestly, and constructively.

____ 0–25% of the time   ____ 51–75% of the time

____ 26–50% of the time   ____ 76–100% of the time

Example:

_____

_____

_____

_____

_____

_____

Communicates appropriately given the situation, not just by e-mail.

____ 0–25% of the time   ____ 51–75% of the time

____ 26–50% of the time   ____ 76–100% of the time

Example:

_____

_____

_____

_____

_____

_____

Is nondefensive and open to feedback, and takes responsibility for miscommunication.

_____ 0–25% of the time   _____ 51–75% of the time

_____ 26–50% of the time   _____ 76–100% of the time

Example:

_____

_____

_____

_____

_____

_____

Communicates well with other departments and respects others' communication styles.

_____ 0–25% of the time   _____ 51–75% of the time

_____ 26–50% of the time   _____ 76–100% of the time

Example:

_____

_____

_____

_____

_____

_____

5. Personal Leadership

Demonstrates the ability to take responsibility for decisions and actions.

____ 0–25% of the time   ____ 51–75% of the time

____ 26–50% of the time   ____ 76–100% of the time

Example:

_____

_____

_____

_____

_____

Sets high standards for himself/herself.

____ 0–25% of the time   ____ 51–75% of the time

____ 26–50% of the time   ____ 76–100% of the time

Example:

_____

_____

_____

_____

_____

Demonstrates a proactive and positive attitude toward business and colleagues.

_____ 0–25% of the time   _____ 51–75% of the time

_____ 26–50% of the time   _____ 76–100% of the time

Example:

_____

_____

_____

_____

_____

_____

_____

Demonstrates professional behavior in interactions with all employees.

_____ 0–25% of the time   _____ 51–75% of the time

_____ 26–50% of the time   _____ 76–100% of the time

Example:

_____

_____

_____

_____

_____

_____

Is willing to do whatever is needed to get the job done.

____ 0–25% of the time   ____ 51–75% of the time

____ 26–50% of the time   ____ 76–100% of the time

Example:

_____

_____

_____

_____

_____

Leads by example and is an inspiration to others in the workplace.

____ 0–25% of the time   ____ 51–75% of the time

____ 26–50% of the time   ____ 76–100% of the time

Example:

_____

_____

_____

_____

_____

Copyright Synthesis at Work

In *6 Habits of Highly Effective Bosses,* authors Stephen E. Kohn and Vincent D. Connell say the following with regard to 360-degree reviews:

> A 360 degree feedback project encourages individuals to rate themselves on certain widely acknowledged dimensions of leadership and/or personal effectiveness, while also encouraging ratings on the same dimensions from a select group of those familiar with the individual (subordinates, peers, bosses and sometimes customers) using the same rating scale. In this way an average rating from a group of others can be compared to the individuals self-rating to identify differences (if any) in these perceptions and uncover potential blind spots. The goal is to help an individual perform an accurate self-assessment.

Now, at this point you may be asking yourself, *How often should I or our organization be conducting a 360-degree review?* Typically it is recommended every other year, which allows for implementation of the results, but also takes into consideration staff changes and any changes within the organization. The perfect circumstances to create the 360-degree review system are when undergoing organizational change, new focus, and direction, or with leaders who have been on the job for a lengthy time and need to adapt to new direction. Dynamic organizations that continue to provide training and learning to their leaders and their teams recognize the benefits of a 360 review process.

In a perfect world a successful 360 program would result in senior management and leaders making positive changes in how they each function individually. As a result of the individual shift in behaviors the senior management and the leaders would create new ways of collaborating, brainstorming, and strategizing for higher level outcomes. The international games company that I previously mentioned is an example of an organization that was committed to undertaking the 360 program. I worked with the company for the first two years of the implementation of the program, and the overall results were positive and created better leaders for the organization.

A company that sees the value in developing its leaders through assessment and feedback recognizes competitive benefits. This games company soared far ahead of its competition in terms of attracting high-performing employees, keeping very talented and highly sought leaders from going elsewhere, and creating a work environment that was energetic, accountable, creative, and results-focused. There was no longer a sense of entitlement among employees, but rather a new respect for themselves as individuals as well as for their teammates and their contributions. As a result of attracting and keeping the best people in the business, this company set itself apart from its competitors in the industry and today enjoys increased market share.

What Is a Control Freak to Do if You Don't Like the Feedback?

I don't care how evolved you are. Hearing feedback still causes even the best of us to want to get defensive. Let's say your 360 comes back saying you are highly controlling, impatient, condescending, and overbearing. (I had that feedback in my early years as a leader.) You have two choices: First, you can be angry and justify the behavior, or second, you can see the feedback from someone else's perspective and choose to shift your behavior to help you accomplish better results.

In my case if I were honest, yes, I was all of the descriptors listed, and yet I was also highly effective at what I did. I got the results, and my customers loved my efficiency, but my teammates didn't love me.

I decided that my desire to be a better leader was more important than my need to defend my behaviors. Of course, I didn't change overnight—no one does—but I did begin to shift my approach, and I also began to own up to my negative behaviors when I went to use them.

I had one leader who was so focused on protecting his title and his identity as a high-powered leader that he just wasn't willing to receive the 360 feedback. I had empathy for him, because he had built his success to date on his skills. However, he was also hindering the company's growth from $50 million to $100 million, which was his goal. My strategy was not to convince him that the feedback was right, but instead asked him to think about why 10 of his direct reports would have such similar perceptions. Was it possible that there was a kernel of truth in the feedback? I gave him a week to sit with that, and at our next meeting he had completely shifted his attitude around the feedback he had received. He humbly acknowledged that, because he hadn't been "called on" the behavior before the 360, he justified his approach as being successful. Once he had a chance to assimilate the feedback, he got very excited and decided to use the information to grow himself to the next level. This executive's direct report could not get over his dramatic change within a three-month period. He spent more one-on-one time with his leaders, he held regular "fireside chats" where anyone could ask him anything, and he began to poke fun at his failings in front of his team to show that he knew his areas for development and that he was working on them.

The organization shifted dramatically, as if often does when senior management makes dramatic changes in their approach, and it went on to become the industry leader.

It's up to you and the organization as to whether or not you see any merit in implementing a 360 program, but I can tell you it is a bold company who is willing to do it, hear the results, and then make changes around the outcomes of the process.

You can bet that the most successful leaders have had to hear very difficult feedback or opinions in their journey to the top. In Chapter Nine we will look at the most maddening behaviors of control freaks and how we use them to our advantage.

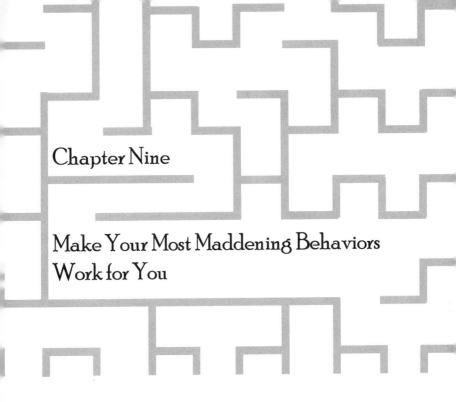

Chapter Nine

Make Your Most Maddening Behaviors Work for You

I live in my own little world, but it's okay. They know me here.

—Anonymous

Okay, so you have read this far and you are willing to change some of your behaviors. Good for you! But there are some fundamental behavioral traits that you just can't envision being able to change that quickly. After all, it took you many years to end up the way you are.

In her new book *Megatrends 2010: The Rise of Conscious Capitalism*, author Patricia Aburdene talks about "self-mastery." Aburdene, as you'll recall, is the best-selling author of *Megatrends 2000* and *Reinventing the Corporation*. She asks, "How can you control your environment if you can't even manage your own thoughts and emotions? In other words, how do you rule the world without first mastering yourself?"

We can be masters of our behaviors. Let's look at the most maddening behaviors of a self-confessed control freak and see how you can turn them around to serve you and the people around you.

The most maddening behaviors of a control freak are:

→ Impatient.

→ Overbearing.

→ Over-controlling or micromanaging.

→ Condescending.

→ Don't trust anyone but yourself.

→ Can't stand others' incompetence.

→ Perfectionist.

→ Pushy and forceful.

Some of them they aren't so flattering, and yet there are some merits to these control freak behaviors that we can use to our advantage.

Let's go through each of these and identify some strategies that you can use to turn the maddening control freak behaviors into a positive for you in your work and in your life.

Maddening Behavior: Impatient

When someone is impatient it can be a very good thing. Impatience is the impetus to change; the opposite of impatience is complacency. A control freak would argue that complacency is worse than impatience. However a control freak can justify being impatient, it clearly can be an irritating behavior to others.

The key is to use your tendency to be impatient for good. When we feel our impatience in wanting to make positive change, this can be an impetus for growth. When we impose our impatience on others or expect others to have our same sense of urgency, this can be a most maddening behavior.

Many competitive organizations use impatience as a positive in product development. For example, in the technology sector many new products are brought to market as a result of impatience. As a leader, being impatient can push products or services to change quickly, but it can also cause others to push back at us. Previously I mentioned that we need to adapt to the different personality styles of those who report to us, those we report to, our customers, and our suppliers. Use your impatience for good, recognize when you are feeling impatient, name it, and let others know why you are impatient with this particular item or situation. Clarify when you are feeling impatient with a particular person. Explain to him/her your reasons for wanting to rush something and ask him/her to cooperate with your request for speed. Take the time to understand the personality of the person you are dealing with. Recognize when your impatience is irrational and irritating, and adjust your behavior accordingly. Others can see impatience as maddening, but you can use it to your advantage by recognizing the merits and the pitfalls of the behavior and adjusting yourself as needed.

Questions to ask yourself when you are feeling impatient include:

→ Why am I feeling urgency around this issue?

→ Is it my need to control, or are there valid reasons for my need for speed?

→ Have I provided the other person with the information he/she needs so that we are on the same page and we can move ahead quickly?

→ Will I get any further ahead if I push at this?

→ How can I communicate to others my rationale for being impatient on this issue and get them to side with me?

Maddening Behavior: Overbearing

In my early days as a leader I thought overbearing meant authoritative. I did not have the emotional intelligence to know that it was a maddening behavior that made others feel belittled.

People who are overbearing are exhausting. Overbearing behavior is forceful, powerful, and makes others feel small. The definition of overbearing from the dictionary is:

1. *Domineering; dictatorial; haughtily or rudely arrogant.*

2. *Of overwhelming or critical importance.*

Overbearing behavior stems from the same insecurities as the other behaviors of a control freak. We are afraid that if we do not show strong authority then we will not be taken seriously or we may lose our power. Typically the behavior backfires, because it is a behavior that pushes others away rather than brings them toward us. When we push people away with our behaviors we create an emotional divide where we cannot work together cooperatively. Rather, we create division and separation.

The key to making this maddening behavior work for you is to shift the negative elements of being overbearing into a collaborative approach that gains respect from others. When we consistently use overbearing behavior we are perceived as assholes. Yep, I used the word—but not before it was already used in a best-selling book by Robert I. Sutton, PhD: *The No Asshole Rule—Building a Civilized Workplace and Surviving One That Isn't.*

In his book Sutton says being in control is at the center of being perceived as a jerk. He states that control is a positive need for all people including those with whom we are being overbearing. In an excerpt he states:

Rigorous research confirms that the feeling of control—perceiving that you have the power to shape even small aspects of your fate—can have a huge impact on human well-being. Consider a compelling study by Ellen Langer and Judith Rodin with elderly patients in nursing homes. One group of patients attended a lecture about all the things the staff could do for them; they were given a houseplant and told the staff would care for it, and they were told which night to attend movies. Patients in the other (quite similar) groups from the same nursing homes were given a 'pep talk' about the importance of taking care of the new houseplant in their rooms, and given choices about which nights to attend movies, when they had meals, when their phones rang, and how their furniture was arranged. These small differences had big effects. Not only did those whose patients with greater control engage in more recreational activities and have more positive attitudes toward life in general, an eighteen month follow-up found that they had a 50% lower death rate.

As a control freak, if you shift your overbearing tendencies to providing choice to others, you will see a positive shift in their attitudes and responses to your leadership. Ask yourself the following questions to check in on your overbearing behavior:

→ι What am I afraid of losing if I am not overbearing?

→ι What beliefs do I have about myself and my value compared to others and their value?

→ι What can I do when I feel myself behaving in an overbearing way?

→ı Do I have the courage to apologize or admit my behavior in order to build better relationships and collaboration?

Maddening Behavior: Over-Controlling or Micromanaging

I really believe the intentions of someone who wants to micromanage are really very good. Often the person who wants to over-control has had to "take control" in many areas of his/her life, and that behavior has spilled over into his/her leadership style. Someone who must control or micromanage typically believes that no one else can do it right, no one else can do it as fast, and it won't get done if we don't do it. Sound familiar?

Over-controlling on a personal level will always create unnecessary stress. My best friend since high school, Sue, is a highly accomplished professional. She is a leader in the field of group insurance and is highly respected. Sue got to where she is today because she has taken control of every aspect of her life. Recently, though, Sue found that her need to over-control cost her sleep and needless worry. A pipe burst in her building, damaging several condos, including Sue's, forcing her to relocate temporarily. Her temporary housing was rented to someone else before she could return to her condo, and Sue learned she had just a week to find a new place to live.

She went in to her "control" mode and began to frantically search for another furnished apartment. None were available, and her stress level went into overdrive. I asked her why the insurance company wasn't looking for an apartment for her, and Sue said, "Because I have to do this or I won't have a place to live." Long story short, her stay was extended until she could return home and Sue finally realized that, had she put the problem back on the insurance company, she would have experienced less stress. Control sneaks up on us, and we may not even see that our need to control is causing us excess stress and worry. The challenge with any of us who have felt the need to be in control because no one else will do it for us is that we can sabotage allowing others to step in and do what they are supposed to do in the situation.

The fact is that being in control is a necessary strength of a great leader. We need to get better at discerning what is worth controlling and what can we allow others to do for us. We can shift this maddening behavior into a major advantage in the way we control, in the way we empower others to control, and in sharing the control.

I worked as a volunteer on a national board for three years and prior to that another four years on the local board with the same organization. I was president of the association last year, and one of my responsibilities was to oversee the annual convention. My convention chair, Elaine, is a control freak's dream: She is a planner, she gets it done, and she is fantastic at follow-up. The only challenge we had is that we are both highly controlling and we had a few disagreements along the way. At one point we had to have a conversation about her stepping in to do things that had been assigned to others. When that happened, others on the volunteer team would then simply "give up" because Elaine was going to do it for them anyway.

In her heart Elaine's intentions were good, and it was extremely difficult for her to wait for others to fulfill their commitments to the project. Being a micromanager is good in that everything gets done—BUT it can cause apathy and team malaise as the team realizes its over-controlling leader will end up saving the day anyway. Now I wish I could say that I was not over-controlling, but that would be a lie. I had such a strong vested interest in making the 10th annual convention a huge success and so did Elaine. I had to examine my intentions, and then state to Elaine and her team why we were over-controlling certain aspects and also "trusting" that the team would follow through on all of the other aspects. We both turned our over-controlling and micromanaging behaviors to our advantage by stating what we were going to continue to micromanage and what we were going to give to the team. The team actually respected our commitment to high quality and "allowed" us to micromanage a few segments, but then stepped up big-time in following through on its responsibilities. When you find yourself being overly controlling ask yourself the following questions:

→ Am I really the ONLY one who can do this part?

→ What would happen if I took the time to go over this with the team? Could the team do it?

→ Why do I feel the need to micromanage this project?

→ Am I willing to come clean with my team and admit I am being overly controlling and why?

→ What could I do to begin trusting my team members more and let them have more control?

Maddening Behavior: Condescending

Do you ever watch *Hell's Kitchen* on TV? Chef Gordon Ramsay is arrogant, condescending, and overbearing, and yet he has kept the same staff with him for years. The following condescending statement, found online, is from Gordon Ramsay himself:

> My staff is mostly long-serving, which is very unusual in professional kitchens where there tends to be a very fast turnover of staff. There are a big percentage of people out there who've seen me on the TV and who think I'm an

arsehole. That's fine; the people who come up with this crap have never worked for me, and obviously haven't bothered talking to anyone who has. I don't give a damn if some dental hygienist comes up to me and tells me that she would never tolerate my behavior from her boss—or behave in similar fashion to someone in her employ. Kitchens are not like other workplaces. People who've worked with me, and who have survived, love it. I'm not speaking on their behalf—but ask them, and you'll see that I'm right. What they get from me is brutal honesty, and that's paramount.

Gordon Ramsay is right: Running a kitchen is not exactly the same as running another business, except that he has put his most maddening behaviors to work for him and his staff. The people who would enjoy working for Gordon Ramsay would expect him to be over-controlling and a perfectionist, and they would also expect to learn a lot from him. On the show he comes across as terribly condescending and yet it reminds me of a drill sergeant who has to ensure that the team "gets it" so in situations of life or death, the "rules" are already established. Now, cooking is not life or death—but it is to Chef Gordon Ramsay.

How can you shift condescending into "teaching" so that others appreciate your expertise, experience, and knowledge? Condescending behavior is not just the words that you choose; it is very much about the *way* you say it that can be maddening. Let others know up front that patience is not your virtue, that you know the function of the job you are trying to teach them inside and out, AND that teaching others to do it exactly the way you do it is your goal (although a challenging task at the best of times). A lot of control freaks feel they are the only ones who can teach others what they know, but there are huge advantages to having others teach and train, cross-training within the department, and providing your team with the tools they need in order to do their jobs well.

Here are some questions to ask yourself when you are behaving in a condescending way:

→ı Why am I treating this person in a disrespectful way?

→ı Have I personally taken the time to first communicate my high expectations and then to train and teach others to meet my high expectations?

→ı Do I need to be rude or belittling in order to get my point across?

→ı How would the workplace be if I were more respectful, tolerant, and patient with others?

→ı What would I personally gain from being more appreciative and tolerant?

Maddening Behavior: Don't Trust Anyone but Yourself

This behavior is the one that keeps good managers from being great, and it keeps entrepreneurs from growing their businesses to the next level. I am guilty of this one big-time. I have been self-employed now for 13 years, and one of the aspects of being an entrepreneur that I enjoy is the ability to "control" my time, output, and environment. However, as do most who are in business for themselves, I hit the wall of no growth a few years ago. I was holding on to controlling all aspects of my business so that I could know what was going on, not have to answer to anyone else, and keep it nice and manageable. I realized when I sat down with my business coach and my accountant that I had to give up control of certain areas of my business if I was going to get it to the level of business that I wanted.

Two years ago I hired a virtual assistant and a marketing group to take away the administrative duties I was getting bogged down with. When I examined why I kept doing the administrative duties I realized it was easy and comfortable, and I had fallen into a routine doing them. In truth it was keeping me from spending time doing the high-value activities, such as talking to potential clients, following up on referrals, and writing this book, along with many other high-energy projects.

When I dug even deeper into why I hadn't passed these parts of my business on earlier it was because I was worried that my clients only wanted to deal with me directly and that I might lose business if someone else was their contact point. I didn't trust anyone but myself. This is not so much a maddening behavior to us although it can have negative consequences; it is a maddening behavior for others when we do not trust them. We can turn this maddening behavior into an advantage by slowly letting go of our high need to control and begin to let our team prove to us it is worthy and up to the tasks.

In my case, Karen, my marketing manager, knows I am a recovering control freak and I admit when I am feeling "out of control." This allows her to not take it personally when I question an action or suggest a different approach for future. Having an over-inflated ego can be a control freak's downfall BUT it can also lead to huge success. Gene Simmons of KISS fame comes off as a highly egotistical freak on the reality show *Family Jewels,* but look at what he has created! I love this quote from him on the show:

> Let's face it, just because I stick out my tongue a lot and spit fire doesn't mean I have any qualifications to advise anyone on relationship, money, or career issues. I don't. Yet I've lived with a beautiful woman for 20 years with never

> a cross word between us, in a relationship based on honesty and full disclosure. I've amassed a fortune—and "expert business people" work for me. And for three decades I've been in KISS—a band that has scaled the heights and broken every possible record, from album sales to touring to merchandising and licensing. What I have and have always had (thanks in full to my mother's wisdom) is an abiding faith in me. Call it a "life philosophy": a philosophy about money (mine!) and happiness (mine again). It works for me. It can work for you!

Notice that although he asserts he has a strong ego he also admits he has "expert businesspeople" who work for him. He has learned the power of giving away areas of control.

Here are some more questions about trust:

→ Why do I have trouble trusting others?

→ What am I afraid of losing if I give up control to others?

→ What is the worst-case scenario if I give up control of certain aspects of my job or business?

→ What skills would I need to develop if I were to delegate more?

→ Do I use the statement "I have no time" a lot? (If so, when am I choosing to make the time?)

Maddening Behavior: Can't Stand Others' Incompetence

A control freak has zero tolerance for when others make mistakes. This is a maddening behavior to others, because we always make them out to be schmucks, idiots, or incompetent baboons. We may not even be aware that we are doing this controlling behavior. We can actually turn this maddening behavior into an advantage and become an extraordinary teacher and mentor that inspires others to high performance.

In the story about Chef Gordon Ramsay he has actually set an expectation that he will not suffer fools and that those who choose to work for him better have tough skin. In most corporate environments, however, the same behavior would be barbaric. The scary thing is that there are stories out there of corporate bosses behaving in the same way and getting away with it.

When you think about it, the root of not being able to tolerate others' incompetence comes from an internal standard that is nothing less than perfection. We need to define incompetence for ourselves. We need to also ask ourselves if we have provided the training, support, and knowledge that the team needs in order to perform at its highest levels possible. If it's not a team but another individual, we have to take a deep breath and ask ourselves if we have communicated as clearly as we could to the person who is proving to be an incompetent idiot. We often feel superior and holier than thou when we know that we are masters at something and others around us are not. Behaving as if we are superior and intolerant of others is extremely frustrating and maddening for those around us. We can turn this into a learning advantage for both us and the person we deem as incompetent.

Again it comes down to communication: We can explain our high standards and our frustrations when things are done to our standards. We can reexplain exactly step by step what we want and provide all of the tools for the other person to succeed. Explain to him/her that if it is not done to your standards, you will be asking him/her to do it again until he/she gets it right. It is actually quite motivating to others when we set high standards, hold them to the standards, guide them to meet the expectations, and then reward when they have risen to the challenge.

The next part is more challenging, which is to continue to provide the tools and the guidance when they do not do what we requested to perfection, until they get it right. There is tremendous satisfaction in helping someone master a task; they tend to perform at consistently high levels when we do provide them with what they need to do a stellar job. I don't think people are purposely trying to prove their incompetence to us. I think they are intimidated by highly controlling and perfectionist-type people.

In reality the fact is that, as control freaks, we can't stand others' incompetence. We are really operating from a place of superiority and over-inflated ego. Now, I am the first to admit that, if I am a customer and the person serving me hasn't got a clue, this will push my buttons. Rather than lose it or become condescending I think it's important that we ask ourselves some questions about this:

- → Why am I so annoyed by this person's inability to get it?

- → Is he/she purposely trying to be incompetent?

- → What can I do to support this person so that he/she "gets it"?

- → What are the repercussions of his/her incompetence? Is it life or death?

- → Is it possible that this person just doesn't know and that no one took the time to tell or teach him/her?

Maddening Behavior: Perfectionist

I actually don't see a big problem with wanting perfection! As said by a true recovering perfectionist. There are huge benefits to being a leader who wants to achieve big things that are done with high standards. Studies have shown that leaders who have very high standards create an environment with high morale and quality of output. Actually the opposite attitude of having things just be "okay" can lead to poor quality of work, complacency, and apathy. In my opinion striving for high standards is a perfectly acceptable behavior. Notice though that I used the word *striving*.

As a logical person you and I both know that perfection is near impossible and an out-of-control control freak can drive him/herself to drink if his/her focus is on attaining pure perfection on every task or project. Add to that that those around us can become completely de-motivated, demoralized, and jaded when their production does not meet the perfection standard of a control freak. So how can we turn the maddening behavior of perfection into an advantageous behavior? With lots of practice and by shifting into healthy achiever attitudes and behaviors!

First let's look at the difference between that of a perfectionist and that of a healthy achiever. The perfectionist sets standards beyond reach and is never satisfied with anything less than perfection. A healthy achiever sets high standards that are just beyond reach and enjoys the process as well as the end result. The perfectionist becomes depressed when he/she experiences failure and disappointment. A healthy achiever bounces back from failure and disappointment quickly. A perfectionist has a fear of failure and disapproval. A healthy achiever does not think of failure as bad; rather, he/she sees everything as experience. A perfectionist sees mistakes as evidence that he or she is not worthy. A healthy achiever sees mistakes as learning opportunities. A perfectionist becomes overly defensive when criticized. A healthy achiever reacts positively to healthy feedback. A control freak may make a statement such as, "I wouldn't be where I am today if I weren't such a perfectionist."

One of the characteristics of perfectionists is their rigidity. They refuse to let go of certain ideas even in the face of evidence to the contrary. Here is a parable illustrating the pitfalls of value rigidity, adapted from *Zen and the Art of Motorcycle Maintenance*. The "South Indian Monkey Trap" was developed by villagers to catch the ever-present and numerous small monkeys in that part of the world. It involves a hollowed-out coconut chained at a stake. The coconut has some rice inside, which can be seen through a small hole. The hole is just big enough that the monkey can put his hand in, but it's too small for his fist to come out after he has grabbed the rice. Tempted by the rice, the monkey reaches in and is suddenly trapped. He is not able to see that it is his own fist that traps him—his own desire for the rice. He rigidly holds on the rice, because he values it. He cannot let go and by doing so retain his freedom. So the trap works and the villagers capture him.

Ask yourself the following questions about your need for perfectionism:

→ What are the advantages of trying to be perfect?

→ What are the disadvantages of trying to be perfect?

→ How does my all-or-nothing attitude affect people in my life and at work?

→ Would I still find myself likeable if I wasn't perceived as perfect?

→ How can I shift criticism from making me look bad to helping me to learn and grow?

Maddening Behavior: Pushy and Forceful

A pushy and forceful person is someone who uses highly aggressive behaviors to get his/her way. For others this is a most maddening behavior because it discounts their value as a person and it is intimidating to deal with. We control freaks can turn this into an advantage by shifting pushy and forceful to assertive and influential. You have heard the saying "you can get more bees with honey." Well, we can get better results with assertive and influential when it comes to communicating and leading. When we behave in pushy and forceful ways it almost always is perceived by others as bullying. As a leader, being assertive and influential still challenges others, but in a way that honors who they are as a person.

Earlier in this book I mentioned that people who behave aggressively have self-esteem issues, and that pushy and forceful behaviors are really used to "prove" to the control freak and to others that they are indeed in control. Of course the counterargument is that through the use of fear and intimidation we have used control in a malicious and nonsupportive way. In his book *Reinventing Yourself,* Steve Chandler makes a case for people wanting to be stretched. This excerpt explains that even an amoeba prefers a challenge:

> People look forward to retirement because they imagine great comfort. What they often get is an increase in visits to the doctor, an increase in prescriptions, sometimes an increase in depression and often an early death. The human system does not really want comfort, it wants challenge. It wants adventure. And perhaps we can extend that from the "human system" to *all living beings.*
>
> Stewart Emery reports a startling experiment done with amoebas in California. In his book *Actualizations,* he reveals how two tanks of amoebas were set up in order to study the conditions most conducive to growing living organisms.
>
> In one tank, the amoebas were given ultimate comfort. The temperature, humidity and

water levels, and other conditions were constantly adjusted for ultimate ease in living and proliferation. In the other tank, the amoebas were subjected to rude shocks. They were given rapidly whipsawing changes in fluid level, temperature levels, protein, and every other condition they could think of. To the total amazement of the researchers, the amoebas in the more difficult conditions grew faster and stronger than those in the comfort zone. They concluded that having things too set and too perfect can cause living things to decay and die, whereas adversity and challenge lead to strength and the building of life force.

This story illustrates that stretching others to grow and perform at higher levels is what causes stimulation, excitement, energy, and growth. Being assertive and influential challenges others but in a way that supports them to grow. Do you have a dog? My golden retriever, Maya, responds very well to assertive but not so well to forceful. Why? Because dogs respond to pack leader energy that is calm, focused, and in positive control. Not to compare humans to dogs, but I see many similarities in how we teach our dogs and how we can get people to respond in a positive way. Here are some questions to ask yourself about turning pushy and forceful into assertive and influential:

→| How can I say what I am about to say in a way that is assertive and influential?

→| Why do I feel the need to be pushy or forceful about this?

→| What could I gain if I shifted my behavior to assertive and influential?

➔ What could I do as a reminder to myself to switch my behavior when I am behaving in a pushy and forceful way?

There you have it: how to turn your most maddening behaviors in your advantage. If you got this far and you were willing to admit to some of the negative behaviors of a freaky control freak, then in my opinion you are halfway there! I find myself enjoying the growing journey so much from shifting my negative behaviors into positive—and the people in my life and work are enjoying it, too!

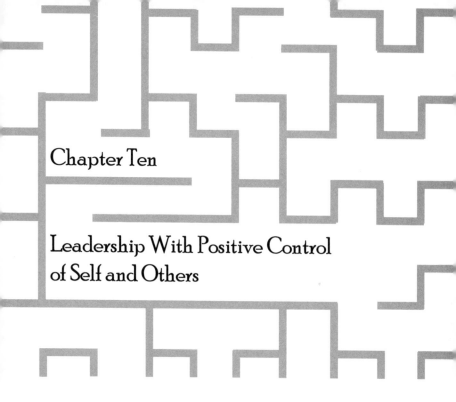

Chapter Ten

Leadership With Positive Control of Self and Others

He who controls others may be powerful, but he who has mastered himself is mightier still.

—Tao Te Ching

The art of mastering control for positive results is one that takes time, introspection, experience, and a willingness to learn and grow. Throughout this book we have looked at the elements of being a positive control freak. To wrap it all up let me share with you some stories of leaders who have made the shift away from nasty control freakiness to positive and results-oriented control.

I worked with a division of KPMG a few years ago and was conducting a leadership retreat. KPMG has done an excellent job of identifying the requirements for its leaders to be successful in their roles. At this leadership retreat we were identifying the positive characteristics of a fantastic leader, and near the top of the list of characteristics was a leader who could take "control" in a positive and purposeful way. The personality aspects that were listed included *approachable, likeable, focused,* and *inspiring.*

When we took a break I had the pleasure of sitting next to a gentleman, Gary, who was open, connecting with everyone at the table, congenial, and yet had an imposing presence. He was more than 6 feet tall and fairly substantial in size. My intuitive sense was that he was highly loved by all because of his demeanor. I also sensed though that he was a take-charge, head-into-battle-and-win kind of guy. I asked the CFO who I was sitting beside and how many of KPMG's "top" leaders were present at the retreat. He responded that every single one of their leaders was present. I then asked about Gary, and he smiled and said, "He is one of our superstars."

I had suspected as much but I went on to ask the CFO to give me specific traits that Gary exhibited to make him a superstar leader. The CFO said, "He is a go to the wall for his team, strongly opinionated control freak—but in a good kind of way." In fact Gary modeled the KPMG "brand" of a good leader. One of the things Gary does as a leader is to control his environment every Monday morning. He establishes a pep talk for his entire team and lets the team know what needs to be under control for the week, and then reminds everyone that he is a control freak and wants to ensure all goals for the week are accomplished. He rewards his team at the end of the week with a wrap-up pep talk and individual recognition in front of the entire team. The team members respond to him because he truly cares about them, but he is committed to controlling the team's commitment to getting results. In this example Gary has learned to harness the positive elements of being in control and has created a team who aspire to model his leadership.

Consider Randy and Tim from Renaissance Homes, the CEO and CFO, respectively, from earlier in the book. Both are strong control freaks, and both acknowledge that they have had to adapt their approach in order to get better results. Before I came along as their consultant they were doing fantastic business. The challenges they were having were with people management and disagreement about the direction of the company. They had leveled off at a respectable 200 homes a year but wanted to grow to 400 homes in two years. When I met Randy at a convention, he knew that his need to control was causing the company some unnecessary pain, and he wanted to shift his control in a positive way.

Randy has grown the business from the ground up in 20 years. He started with nothing and went from building each home himself to now having more than 30 builders and many more sub-contractors building the homes for the company. Randy himself states that the turning point for his business came in the early 1990s when his company took a major nosedive. It was at that time he realized he needed to let go of control of certain aspects of the business, and that is when he made the smartest business decision of his life and hired Tim. Randy put Tim in control of financing and operations, and that was the beginning of the next phase of the company. The biggest challenge for any company is when it has to make the transition from small and manageable to bigger and more standardized. Many business owners resist this transition because they don't want to lose the familial feel of the company or they fear that the bigger the company gets the more they will lose control.

The key to next level growth for an organization is shifting the focus and the activities away from what has been done as a smaller company and into new methods of operation. Randy and Tim realized that standardization of processes was inevitable if they were to get the company to the size and scope that they wanted. When it comes to people management, this means having systems in place to support the career path, job scope, and performance evaluation. Most small companies have what I call default people-management practices. In other words, they do what they have to do (such as payroll, vacation administration, and benefits). The challenge is that everything around the people management is so casual that there can be an attitude of familiarity and nonaccountability. Tim's leadership style as CFO is very much about controlling costs, controlling purchases, and ensuring financial stability for the company. Randy's style is to buy land, buy more land, and worry about what to do with the land at a later date. Together they are a dynamo, and they both knew they could leverage their individual control styles to get the company to grow.

It is very difficult to convince highly successful and controlling people that they need to shift their behaviors. In this case I was not in a position to tell them that what they had been doing up until the point of bringing me on was wrong. Instead I asked them if they were willing to look at shifting their control so that they could create the results they wanted. The shift that needed to happen was to look at what was working and what was holding growth at bay. What was working was having Tim in charge of the financing and operations and having Randy in charge of land acquisition. However, at this stage of the game each of them needed to use the resources he had, which were his people.

I mentioned earlier that one of the toughest things for a control freak to do is to delegate, and that was one of the biggest challenges with Tim. When someone is highly talented at particular things, he/she will resist giving those things up (because they make him/her feel successful). Or he/she will create scenarios where the person they delegate to fails and therefore validates his/her concerns that no one can do the job right but the control freak him/herself. A good example of this was the controller Tim had hired. He knew in his gut that she wasn't the exact fit, but he hired her anyway. When I came along I pointed out that the very things he needed from his controller she was not capable of providing, and he was not willing to train her because he didn't like her!

Once we dealt with the right hire and brought in Bruce in the role of controller, things began to shift for Tim, and he became more comfortable in letting some of his duties go. Tim is a highly respected and feared leader. I say feared because he is so smart that he makes anyone around him feel like a kindergartner. I have worked with him to point out that no one wants to let him down and that's why people are afraid to step up for him. One of his direct reports, Marc, is a clone of Tim because he was hired at the beginning with Tim and learned everything from the school of Tim. Marc can go toe to toe with Tim, and he works his butt off, which gains him major brownie points with Tim. The challenge is that others who report to Tim are not clones, requiring Tim to be a positive control freak to get the results he wants from his other reports.

The good news is that when a control freak can see the merits of shifting his/her controlling to a more positive and inspiring way, it has more impact. We standardized the performance review system, and the first formal reviews were met with appreciation by the staff, and it infused new clarity for the leadership team. Tim resisted us going to what he calls "Big Co." (short for "big company") because he had left big corporate to come and work for small and familial. He now admits that there are standardizations that do need to happen so that everyone is on the same page and they can positively "control" their direction.

Randy, on the other hand, recognized that his controlling had worked up to a certain point, but it was time to be strategic about his land acquisition. He has an incredible eye for land, but now that he has 100 people who have to deal with the realities of the land purchase, he is thinking a little differently about what he sees as a fit. Ultimately if land is purchased but there has been little thought to the development challenges, it can cause chaos for the construction team when it comes time to build. Randy liked to control the purchase of land and has seen the benefit of involving Jeff (his land division guy), Tim (his finance guy), and the entire team of construction leaders.

These are two leaders who are both highly controlling, which got them good results, and who have moved their control to focus on the positive aspects of control, such as systemized people management and collaborative strategy planning, which is giving them great results.

> *I am a nobody, nobody is perfect, and therefore*
> *I am perfect.*
>
> —Anonymous

Pink magazine, a business magazine aimed at women, recently profiled a high-achieving control freak named Mellody Hobson. She is a positive control freak in every sense, as she controls her health, her wellness, and her business success. Every morning when she's not traveling Mellody wakes up at 3:50 a.m. to check her Blackberry and then runs on her treadmill for 45 minutes, followed by an hour with her personal trainer. She goes on to say that for her there is no such thing as balance—for her, working and living are balance. She is president of Ariel Capital Management and Ariel Mutual Funds, and chairman of Ariel Mutual Funds' board. Melody is 38 years old and is one of the highest-ranking women in the mutual funds industry. According to the article, she leads fearlessly, acts courageously, and knows who she is and the merits of positive control.

Jennifer Openshaw is another powerful woman who took control of her life and her financial future. I read an interesting piece in *Success* magazine about her that made me think that she is definitely using positive control in her life. Openshaw grew up believing that her success rested squarely on her own shoulders. She was on her own much of her childhood taking care of her brothers and setting a vision for herself of financial independence. When it came time for college Openshaw put herself through school. She saved up, took advantage of scholarships, and worked during her freshman year at Pepperdine University. Openshaw was forced to leave Pepperdine for financial reasons, but she remained determined. She said to herself, "There's no way I'm not going to get a college education. There's nothing you can't do; it's how you go about doing this." She saved her money and set her sights on UCLA and soon enrolled there.

⌐∷⌐

The key components I have discovered in all successful people is that they have a strong inner drive and a vision to create, but they also take full responsibility and control over their lives. They don't wait for others to do it for them, and they have learned to funnel their negative control traits into more positive and successful skills. A number of years ago I worked with the Santa Monica Bay Physicians group. I was hired by a dynamo of a woman named Erin, and she had a very passionate, clear vision of what she and the doctors wanted their practice to be: They wanted their environment and their people to be focused on caring and service, and they wanted to take care of their staff. I was hired to facilitate a session on change as at that time they were going through a major shift in how they were to do business. In the session we had all of the leaders (about 20 of them), and I began to deliver a session on change management.

I sensed that the group was fidgety and uncomfortable, so I took control and said, "Let's put this seminar stuff aside, shall we?" and then I had each leader talk about what he/she felt he/she was losing control of. The results were miraculous in that every leader there felt they were losing control of their voice, of the way they did business, and even possible job loss for some of them.

I then shifted the discussion to what we could control moving forward. As a group we came up with a list of things such as control over current job results, control over maintaining a positive and action-oriented attitude, control over finding new opportunities if they did lose their job, control over going to get further education, and so forth. The meeting ended with each leader realizing that he/she had focused on controlling things that he/she couldn't control, and that this was causing him/her intense stress. By shifting the focus to what each of them actually had control over they all could see that they did have power.

Erin is an amazing HR leader in that she controlled the positive outcomes of the massive changes they had gone through. At the time there were needed restructuring and changes that did happen, and overall the leaders managed the growth to the next level by shifting the focus on what they could control.

In *6 Habits of Highly Effective Bosses*, authors Stephen E. Kohn and Vincent D. O'Connell talk about strong leaders who have the ability to value the differences in people. A funky control freak has learned to do this at very high levels. Here is an excerpt from the book on this:

> The broader frame of reference that managers should assume in assessing people and work issues is that there is value in eliciting different viewpoints about the same situation. The same perspectives on a situation are inherently limiting. One narrow line of vision in assessing something may cause blind spots. Groupthink adds no new information to creative and strategic discussions. Teams that lack diversity often become stagnant and unable to explore exciting and useful alternatives to a problem. So if

managers start their quest to understand the frame of reference of persons who report to them with the attitude that differences are valuable, if not fully understood at all times, it raises the awareness about the need to practice empathy and explore situations in the type of way that the managers themselves would want the situation explored if they felt different from others around them.

If the fact that people are different than you is bothersome to you, it is important to ask yourself: Why this reaction? What is it about the people's differences that you are reacting to? In the workplace context, focused on satisfying customers rather than one's own needs, what differences really exist between people who share an interest in behaving in the customer's best interest?

A freaky control freak will find all differences of opinion from others as something he/she needs to control to make him/her "right." The fact is that opinions are not wrong or right; they are simply opinions. Rather than control the direction or manipulate our own agenda, we can look at differing opinions as a gateway to creative solutions.

A consulting client I have just started working with has grown phenomenally since its inception more than 10 years ago. It is in the staffing industry, and with the current market of the demand for talent the company is extremely busy. The husband-and-wife owners, Trent and Kim, are powerhouses and have high levels of energy, commitment, and drive to keep their company number one in their industry. What struck me right away about the company is that the leaders and most of the employees were all younger than 40. The company has grown because of the energy and passion that Trent and Kim have invested, but the owners also recognize that they have not given more control over to their leaders, and this is causing hiccups as they grow.

Four-wheel drive: The early years.

They have controlled the strategic direction, the growth decisions, and the expansion within their small group of themselves and two other leaders. When working with them, I recommended that they begin to provide control to their leaders in order to include them in the strategy and growth of the company to the next level. Of course you cannot give control without knowing that the people to whom you are giving the power have all of the skills needed to make the right decisions. So the second part of the recommendation was to equip and provide all of the leaders with the necessary training, coaching, and preparation to help take the company to the next growth stage.

Kim and Trent, as team owners, are smart, and they realize that they cannot continue the pace they have been operating at due to life getting in the way. They now have four children, and they also want to be able to not have the company be as reliant on them as it has been in the past. The good news is that they are willing to invest the time, energy, and money to provide structure and put systems in place so that they can have a life while continuing to grow a highly successful business. The reason they have been so successful is because they are both funky control freaks. They figured out that Gen X and Gen Y workers want to have clear goals, lots of fun, big perks, and recognition. The company has attracted high performers because that is the culture that the owners have set. When I interviewed each leader and asked each of them to describe the owners, the words I kept hearing were *passion, energy, commitment, generous, inspiring,* and *controlling but in a good way that's motivating.* On the other hand when I asked the leader what felt they needed to be more successful, the responses were *more control of my responsibilities, more inclusion in strategy planning, support in succession planning,* and *time with the owners so that there could be more knowledge exchange.*

This company has the highly talented people that other companies are longing for, but it risks losing them due the very things mentioned by the leaders that they felt they needed in order to be successful. The leaders are loyal and committed to the owners, and they want to perform at even higher levels.

There is opportunity here for this funky control freak successful business couple to share the control, spread it out, and control from a higher level so that their current leadership can step up and produce results.

In a TV interview Penelope Cruz admitted she had been labeled a control freak. Once again the descriptor she uses is not a negative one; if you read her comments, she definitely comes across to me as a funky control freak. The *Volver* actress, who grew up in a working class Madrid suburb, admits she is a "perfectionist" because her parents always urged her to succeed, but doesn't think she has a problem. She said:

> I've always been a perfectionist, to the point where some people can misinterpret that as being a control freak.
>
> I put more time and energy into something because I want it to be as good as possible. My sister Monica is the same. We are very hard workers. That's how we grew up. My parents taught us that you earn every day that you get. They didn't have a lot of money and they had to work really hard to raise us. So I feel that every opportunity I get, I want to give it 100 percent.

Penelope's comments of how her parents raised her struck me of what environmental factors create elements of a control freak in the first place. In my case, I was raised by a father who insisted I take control of my life. A message I often got growing up was that I had to take control of my life, that no one was going to do it for me, and that no one owed me anything. This was important messaging for me as a young girl, because it caused me to take opportunities wherever I could to achieve what I wanted. The problem is that many of us may not learn the distinction between positive control freak behavior and destructive control freak behavior. In my case I over-compensated in my early 20s to prove that I was in control and that I had control, and my delivery style backfired on me. Once I was able to transform the control freakiness into a positive delivery and learn to distinguish between negative and positive control, I was able to get better results, gain more respect from peers and employees, and create the success I always wanted.

BC Business Magazine is owned by a gentleman named Peter Legge. Peter has made a huge impact on my success as an author and a speaker. We meet for breakfast or lunch on a regular basis, and when we met a few days ago, I mentioned I was in the midst of writing my book on control freaks and he was intrigued. (Peter has written too many books to mention here, but his latest is titled *The Power of Tact*. To find out more go to his Website: *www.peterlegge.com.*) When I talked to Peter about the concept that being a control freak can be a good thing if we are funky not freaky, he loved the idea. I mentioned that he would not be where he is today if he wasn't a control freak, and he agreed. Recently his media company purchased *TV Guide*, and his company is one of the largest media publishing companies in Canada. As my mentor, Peter has demonstrated being a person who has taken full control of his life. He is disciplined in focusing on positive thoughts; he has methodically built his business based on relationships and people skill. He has used positive control in shaping the people who work for him.

What I have learned from Peter is that self-control is the most important element of success. It seems to be a simplistic success principle and yet it is a common factor among highly successful people and leaders. The ability to control self is the absolute foundation in our ability to positively control others.

The common denominator with Rudy Giuliani, Donald Trump, Martha Stewart, Ellen DeGeneres, Oprah Winfrey, and other famous and well-known leaders is that they are all highly controlling of self, success, and others. Viva the Control Freak Revolution!

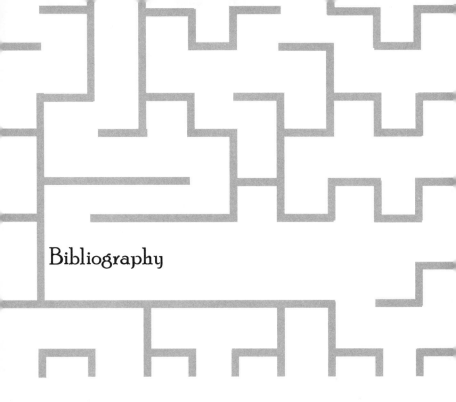

Bibliography

Aburdene, Patricia. *Megatrends 2010: The Rise of Conscious Capitalism.* Charlottesville, Va.: Hampton Roads, 2007.

Buckingham, Marcus. *Now Discover Your Strengths.* New York: The Free Press, 2001.

Byrne, Rhonda. *The Secret.* New York: Atria Books, 2006.

Carlson, Richard D. *Don't Sweat Stories.* New York: Hyperion, 2002.

Chandler, Steve. *Reinventing Yourself.* Franklin Lakes, N.J.: Career Press, 2005.

Chandler, Steve, and Duane Black. *The Hands-Off Manager.* Franklin Lakes, N.J.: Career Press, 2007.

Cran, Cheryl. *Say What You Mean—Mean What You Say.* Victoria, British Columbia: Trafford, 2002.

———. *The Illuminated Leader.* Port Moody, British Columbia: Black Tusk Video, 2006.

Emery, Stewart. *Actualizations.* New York: Doubleday, 1978.

Hartley, Gregory, and Maryann Karinch. *I Can Read You Like a Book.* Franklin Lakes, N.J.: Career Press, 2007.

Hawkins, David. *The Power Vs. Force.* Carlsbad, Calif.: Hay House, 2002.

Kohn, Stephen E., and Vincent D. O'Connell. *6 Habits of Highly Effective Bosses.* Franklin Lakes, N.J.: Career Press, 2005.

Legge, Peter. *The Power of Tact.* Burnaby, British Columbia: Eaglet Publishing, 2007.

Pirsig, Robert M. *Zen and the Art of Motorcycle Maintenance: An Inquiry into Values.* New York: William Morrow and Co., 1974.

Sutton, Robert I., PhD. *The No Asshole Rule—Building a Civilized Workplace and Surviving One That Isn't.* New York: Warner Business Books, 2007.

Wingett, Larry. *It's Called Work for a Reason.* New York: Penguin, 2007.

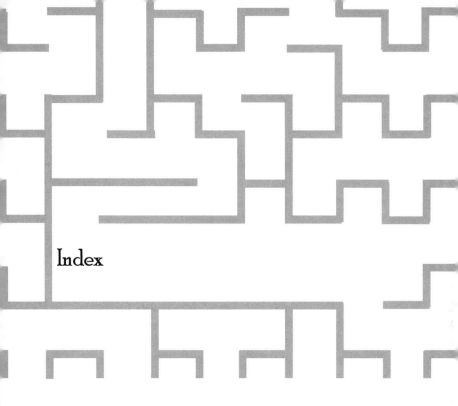

Index

accountability,
    company culture and, 123
    fear of, 123
    positive, 124

action-oriented behavior, 13

action-oriented, the importance of
    being, 40-41

actions,
    employees and negative, 83
    employees and positive, 83
    focusing on positive, 84
    importance of negative, 83
    importance of positive, 83
    taking responsibility
        for, 43

advantage, gaining personal, 118-119

aggressive behavior, negatives of, 24

alert control freak, 42, 52
    strength of a, 45

analysis, opening yourself up to, 133

anti-social behavior, 21

Apprentice, The, 13, 38

archetypes,
    concepts of, 141-143
    personality types and, 142

assertive behavior, negatives of,
    24-25

assertive communication, 61

assertive people, qualities of, 62-63

attitude,
    cultural, 107
    effect of a workplace, 75
    loner, 114, 124-125

aware control freak, 23

awareness,
    expanding your self, 135
    importance of, 22

positive control freak, 138

psychological, 143

situational, 135

Baby Boomer bosses, 101

Baby Boomers, 68, 100, 102

overview of, 103-104

Bagehot, Walter, 18

behavior,

action-oriented, 13

anti-social, 21

condescending, 186-188

control of, 65

focus-oriented, 13

forceful, 195-198

getting rid of

fear-based, 82

impatient, 180-181

micromanaging, 184-86

negative drivers of, 74

overbearing, 182-184

over-controlling, 184-186

perfectionist, 193-194

positive drivers of, 74

pushy, 195-198

questions about

forceful, 197

questions about pushy, 197

behaviors,

becoming masters of our, 180

control and the importance

of, 81

control freak, 14, 180

covert, 29

dealing with negative, 198

destructive, 57

effective, 57

focusing on positive, 22

highly aggressive, 195

identifying team, 154-155

incompetent, 190-192

influence through, 14

shifting, 60

shifting personal, 200

beliefs, list of common, 113-114

Buckingham, Marcus, 38

bullying, control by, 46

challenges, solutions for workplace 65-71

Chandler, Steve, 46-47

change,

managing, 132

resistance to, 111

coaching, importance of, 70

communication gap, bridging the, 66

communication mechanisms,

importance of, 73

organizational, 87

communication,

assertive, 61

control of, 65

frustration with, 191

lack of, 43

communicator, passive, 16

company culture, accountability in the, 123

company morale, factors of, 70

competition rivalry, 119-120

confidence, quiet, 64

conflict situations, control freaks and, 94

conflict, contributions of a control freak to, 93

conscious personal leadership, 143

control freak,

negative, 14

positive, 14

control freak, the term, 13, 16, 36

control,

gaining negative, 119

inspiring others through positive, 145-146

positive aspects of, 74
psyche, 141-143
results-oriented, 199
the importance of
behaviors and, 81
use of time, 143-144
what we can, 18
what we cannot, 18
control panel, successful, 73
controlling behavior,
examples of, 27-28
standing up to, 26-27
controlling mechanism,
self-serving, 40
corporate culture, 111
covert control freak, 29-34, 57 *see
also* freaky control freak
behavior of a, 30
beliefs of a, 30
confronting a, 33-34
dealing with someone
that is, 25
Covey, Stephen, 126-127
coworkers, a negative perception
of, 21
critical analysis, opening yourself
up to, 133
cults, personality, 114-115
cultural differences, controlling, 65
cultural shifts, dealing
with, 129
culture,
corporate, 111
fear-based, 118
organizational, 112
culture change, business, 154
cultures, 107-109
influence through, 14
work ethics of different,
108-109

Dancer personality, 94
elements of a, 99
decision-maker, the importance of
being a, 39-40
decision-making, positive aspects
of, 39
decisions, taking responsibility for, 43
Deflector personality, 94
elements of a, 99
qualities of a, 135
DeGeneres, Ellen, 211
delegation, steps to successful, 144
destructive behaviors, focusing on, 57
Detailer personality, 94
elements of a, 99
differences,
acknowledging
employees', 206
generational, 67-69
personality, 135
discipline, control over, 13
Driver personality, 48, 94, 108
elements of a, 99
qualities of a, 135
effective behaviors, focusing on, 57
ego,
appealing to the, 28-29
dealing with an
over-inflated, 192
employee empowerment,
83, 156
employee, qualities of an ideal, 69
employee retention, 81
employees,
attracting
high-performing, 176
key reasons to keep, 71
solution-oriented, 125

empowerment,
    employee, 156
    importance of
        employee, 83

energy,
    elements of negative
        thought, 77, 83
    elements of negative, 76
    elements of positive
        thought, 83
    elements of positive, 76

environment, high energy, 86

environmental factors, control
    freaks', 210

external situations, getting control
    over, 49

Fanning, Dakota, 41

fear tactics, control by, 46

fear-based behavior, getting rid of, 82

fear-based culture, 118

feedback,
    asking team members
        for, 137
    assertive people and, 63
    getting defensive from, 176
    reactions to, 194
    receiving, 149
    360-degree, 151-155

focus, funky control freaks and, 44-45

focus-oriented behavior, 13

freaky control freak, 23-34
    behavior of a, 24, 30, 58
    beliefs of a, 24, 30
    confronting a, 33-34
    dealing with a, 26-28, 31, 59-61
    description of a, 57-59
    old-style, 47-53
    shifting from a, 77

subconscious behaviors
    of a, 23
the ego and a, 28-29
thoughts of a, 58

funky control freak, 23
    action-oriented, 40-41
    behaviors of a, 61-62
    busting myths of a, 116
    challenges of a, 65
    confronting, 60
    decision-making and
        the, 39
    definition of a, 36
    focus of a, 44-45
    generational differences
        and a, 68
    hiring employees with a, 70
    importance of behaviors
        and a, 83
    interaction with a, 62
    leverage of a, 109
    projections of a, 141
    recognition of a, 38
    risk-taking and the, 41-42
    shifting from a, 77
    strength of a, 45
    thoughts of a, 61-62
    working for a, 60

funky control freak leaders, 63, 100

Gen Xers, 68, 100, 102
    goals of, 209
    overview of, 104-106

Gen Xers in the workforce, 69

Gen Yers, 68, 100, 102
    goals of, 209
    language of, 101
    overview of, 104-106

generation gap, controlling the,
    100-107

generation gaps, workplace conflict
    and, 101

generational differences, 67-69
    funky control freaks and, 68
    influences through, 14
generational values, the workplace
    and, 101-102
generations, differences between,
    100-107
Giuliani, Rudy, 16, 211
hands-on approach, leadership, 44
happiness, what is directly related
    to, 13
Hawkins, David, 79
high-level control freak, 55
highly effective person, 21
high-performing employees,
    attracting, 176
human behavior, positive
    assumptions about, 134-135
human nature, assumptions
    about, 134
incompetence,
    dealing with others', 191
    fear of, 126
influence, media, 18
insecurity, control and, 14
internal rivalry, 119-120
internal thoughts, getting control
    over, 49
job security, 117-118
    leaders and, 118
    myth of, 113
Jobs, Steve, 45, 48
Jung, Carl, 140, 141
Kennedy, John F., 111
knowledge, importance of, 120-122
Kozol, Jonathan, 91

language differences in the
    workplace, 107
leader,
    highly evolved, 135
    self-aware, 134
leader behaviors,
    negative, 37
    behaviors, supportive, 37
leaders,
    assessments for, 160
    control freak, 43
    funky control freak, 100
    funky control freak, 63
    high-performing, 133
    important qualities of, 71
    job security and, 118
leadership,
    adapting to today's, 36
    components of strong, 84
    dictatorial style of, 35
    hands-on approach to, 44
    outcome-based, 87
leadership by control, 35
leadership style, adapting your, 134
likeability factor, 24
Lincoln, Abraham, 138
Lombardi, Vincent, 35
loner attitudes, 124-125
love, as the highest energy point, 77
managers, relationship between
    employees and, 71
manipulation, control by, 46
Mason, John L., 143
mechanisms, organizational
    communication, 87
media, the influence of the, 18
meetings, information-sharing, 127
micromanaging, 184-186

mindset, old-style control freak, 48

mini 360 performance review, 137-138, 151, 155
    sample assessment for a, 160-161

morale, factors of company, 70

myths,
    creating, 111
    creation of, 112
    list of common, 113-114
    negative beliefs and, 112
    organizational, 111, 128
    personal, 111

negative actions,
    employees and, 83
    importance of, 83
    justifications for, 84

negative beliefs, myths and, 112

negative control,
    gaining, 119
    organizations and, 88

negative control freak, 14
    conflict and the, 93

negative energy, elements of, 76

negative energy thoughts, 81

negative leader behaviors, 37

negative perception, giving a, 21

negative thought energy, elements of, 83

nonrecognition, fear of, 122-123

Now Discover Your Strengths, 38

Office, The, 136

old-style control freak mindset, 48

old-style freaky control freak, 47-53

organization,
    existing myths in an, 128
    job security in an, 117

organizational communication mechanisms, 87

organizational control panel, 87
    varying elements of an, 90

organizational culture, 112

organizational myths, 111

organizations, negative control within, 88

outcome-based leadership, 87

outcomes,
    controlling, 74
    focusing on, 84
    four components of, 87-88
    influences of positive, 84-86

overt control freak, 23-29, 57 *see also* freaky control freak
    behavior of a, 24
    beliefs of a, 24

passive-aggressive, control freaks who are, 57

passive-aggressive,
    behavior, 57
    people, 58-59

passive communicator, 16

peer reviews, importance of, 137

perceptions, controlling others', 21-22

perfectionism, questions about, 195

perfectionist behavior, 193-194

perfectionist, healthy achiever versus, 193

performance reviews, standardizing, 74

person, highly effective, 21

personal advantage, gaining, 118-119

personal control panel, 74-87

personal leadership review, setting up a, 158

personal leadership, conscious, 143

personal myths, 111

personalities,
    elements of different, 94-100
    influence through, 14

personality
    cults, 114-115
    differences, 135

personality,
    Dancer, 94
    Deflector, 94
    Detailer, 94
    Driver, 48, 94
    elements of a Dancer, 99
    elements of a Deflector, 99
    elements of a Driver, 99
    elements of a, Detailer, 99
    traits, 140
    types, archetypes and, 142

personality assessment
    questionnaire, 95-97

personality assessments,
    drawbacks of, 70

positive actions,
    employees and, 83
    focusing on, 84
    importance of, 83

positive behaviors, focusing on, 22

positive control,
    inspiring others through,
        145-146
    maintaining, 23

positive control freak, 14
    awareness of a, 138
    projections of a, 141

positive control freak leader,
    elements of a successful, 133

positive energy, elements of, 76

positive outcomes, influences of,
    84-86

positive thought energy, 83

power, control of, 65

power freaks, 65

Power Vs. Force, The, 79

power words, list of, 80

projection,
    definition of, 139-140
    reflection and, 139

projections,
    funky control freak, 141
    positive control freak, 141

psyche control, 141-143

psychological awareness, 143

Ramsay, Gordon, 186, 191

recognition, knowing how to get,
    38-39

reflection, projection and, 139

retention, employee, 81

risk-taker, strengths in being a, 42

risk-taking, importance of, 41-42

rivalry,
    competition, 119-120
    internal, 119-120

Secret, The, 75

Seinfeld, Jerry, positive outcomes
    for, 84-85

self-aware leader, 134

self-awareness, three principles of,
    133-134

self-control,
    having high levels of, 16
    importance of, 13

self-inflated sense of self, 25

self-perception, shifting your, 135

self-serving controlling
    mechanism, 40

self-starters, time and, 126

sense of self, self-inflated, 25

skill sets, identifying gaps in team, 154

solution-oriented employees, 125

Stewart, Martha, 16, 44, 48, 211

strengths,
    building on, 18
    control freak, 38, 57

supportive leader behaviors, 37

Tao Te Ching, 199

techniques, assertive, 60

technology, gaps created by, 67

Thoreau, Henry David, 55

thought energy, appreciation as a, 77

thought energy scale, 76

thoughts,
    importance of, 75-76
    internal, 49
    negative energy, 81

360 performance reviews, 151, 158-159, 175

360-degree evaluation questionnaire, 162-174

360-degree feedback, delivering, 155-156

360-degree performance evaluation, 48

360-degree program, steps to a successful, 156-157

time control, use of, 143-144

time, wasting company, 126-129

training,
    necessities of proper, 66
    strong leadership, 84
    wasted experience of, 66

traits, personality, 140

Truman, Harry, 136

Trump, Donald, 16, 38-39, 41-42, 48, 131, 211

trust,
    issues with, 188-190
    lack of, 119

trust, questions to ask about, 190

truth, speaking the, 31

Veteran/Traditionalist,
    bosses, 101
    demographic, 69

Veterans/Traditionalists, overview of, 102-103

Walters, Barbara, 16

Williams, Robin, 73

Wilson, Colin, 81

Winfrey, Oprah, 16, 17, 211

Witherspoon, Reese, 46

words, list of, 80

work ethics, different cultures and, 108-109

workforce,
    coaching in the, 70
    on-going training in the, 70
    support in the, 70

workplace challenges, solutions for, 65-71

workplace conflict, generation gaps and, 101

workplace,
    generational values in the, 101-102
    language differences in the, 107

About the Author

CHERYL CRAN, CSP (Certified Speaking Professional) is an internationally renowned speaker and expert in communication and leadership. For more than a decade she has worked with thousands of groups to help them communicate and lead at higher levels.

Cheryl's career in leadership began in her early 20s, when she worked for one of the top five financial institutions in Canada. While there she was promoted to her first leadership role with nine direct reports—all of them older. Cheryl was named top-performing leader every year of her 10-year career with the financial group.

After 10 years as a successful leader with the financial group Cheryl was headhunted from the financial industry to the insurance industry, where she excelled as an area manager for MICC (now GE Capital) and met market penetration targets within two years. Later she headed up a new program for a large credit union, exceeding targets within a 10-month time frame.

Cheryl formed her speaking and consulting practice in 1994 and has enjoyed tremendous success as a speaker, facilitator, and consultant to many of North America's top-performing organizations. Clients include KPMG, Price Waterhouse-Coopers, Grant Thornton LLP, CMHC, 3M, Care 1st Health, the Motion Picture Association, the U.S. Navy Reserve, Chevron, and many more.

She holds certificates in communication, leadership, neuro-linguistic programming, and psychology.

Cheryl holds the Certified Speaking Professional designation. (Only 10 percent of speakers worldwide who are members of the International Federation of Speakers hold this designation.) Her expertise is in communication, leadership, and lifelong learning. She is the author of *50 Ways to Lead & Love It* and *Say What You Mean—Mean What You Say*, as well as a contributing author to *Don't Sweat Stories* and *Speak Up— Speak Out*.

Cheryl has delivered thousands of presentations to companies since 1994 and has worked with hundreds of companies as a consultant.

To contact Cheryl and find out more about working with her, please go to *www.cherylcran.com*.